ACCESS ALL AREAS

ACCESS ALL AREAS

•

THE DIVERSITY MANIFESTO FOR TV AND BEYOND

•

**LENNY HENRY
& MARCUS RYDER**

faber

First published in 2021
by Faber & Faber Limited
Bloomsbury House
74–77 Great Russell Street
London WC1B 3DA

Typeset by Faber & Faber Limited
Printed and bound by CPI Group (UK) Ltd, Croydon, CRO 4YY

A CIP record for this book
is available from the British Library

ISBN 978–0–571–36512–8

2 4 6 8 10 9 7 5 3 1

To Lisa and Hannah

CONTENTS

1

THE PUN THAT CHANGED MY LIFE

Puns are possibly the lowest form of humour. I know people say sarcasm is the lowest form of wit, but finding something funny just because two words sound vaguely similar is really very stupid. Sometimes, *I love being very stupid* and some pun-tastic stuff works a treat. For example, I renamed my iPod The Titanic so that when I plug it in it says 'The Titanic is syncing'. (Get it? Syncing sounds like 'sinking' – and the *Titanic* sank, right?) But some puns are just embarrassingly silly.

And so it is with a heavy heart that I must admit that it was because of a silly pun, and a tad too much Cinzano Bianco, that I started down the road of battling for a better society. A society that recognises we all have something to offer irrespective of whether we are Black, White, Brown or any other concentration of melanin (see Dulux colour chart for more details). A society where we are all treated fairly regardless of our gender or whether or not we have a disability.

A country where our place of birth, accent or sexual orientation does not determine our future.

My personal journey has been a long, bumpy road, which has involved everything from arguing with my missus about what racism is like in the UK to buttonholing prime ministers at Chequers. (Comic Relief was invited to Chequers by David Cameron. He was all over me like psoriasis. I have no idea why.) But *this* journey started because of a terrible pun. So, I know you are dying to know what this terrible pun was and how it had such a big effect.

Not so fast, amigo. First, a little background . . .

On 12 May 2013, I showered, shaved and then pulled my tuxedo out of the wardrobe, splashed on some fresh cologne (Lynx: Dudley – notes of the canal, Graham Willetts's feet and saveloy and chips), got into a taxi, and headed to the annual BAFTA Television Awards ceremony. I know going to awards ceremonies is a privilege and so it is hard to complain about being there, but as I sat there ploughing my way through the hors d'oeuvres (brie, fig and prosciutto crostini – delicious . . .), watching award after award being handed out, I could feel my temperature rising.

Almost everybody who was on the stage that night, whether they were handing out or receiving an award, was White. Of the more than thirty individual nominations, from Best Leading Actor to the Special Award, there was not one Black or Asian nominee. Of the nominated writers, directors, producers and other key creatives of the winning programmes, all forty-two were White.

I first broke into TV by winning the talent show *New Faces* in 1975. Back then I was almost always the only Black person on set. At the BAFTAs that night, it felt like even though I'd spent forty years working in television, ethnicity-wise nothing had changed.

After eating more hors d'oeuvres and drinking several more free glasses of wine, I went to leave the ceremony. At that point I was approached by a journalist from the *Evening Standard* newspaper, who asked me the most innocent of questions: 'What did you think of the BAFTAs?' Which, if you think about it, is almost the journalistic equivalent of, 'Who's your favourite member of BTS?' or, 'Lockdown's been crap, hasn't it?'

This is when I chose to bust out the fateful pun. In total anger and frustration I said, 'Well, I guess it was . . . all *White* on the night!'

I know, embarrassing right?

Terrible pun. I was simply fed up, tired and I'd

probably had a leetle bit too much to drink. I don't even remember what else I said to the reporter but, oh boy, was I reminded when the next day it made headlines across the UK press.

Cue spinning newspaper headlines just like in the old movies . . .

'BAFTAs were a disgrace for not celebrating
Black talent, says Lenny Henry.' *Telegraph*

'"What were the judges doing?" Lenny Henry
blasts BAFTA for not recognising Black talent
at this year's television awards.' *Daily Mail*

The *Guardian* based an *entire opinion piece* around it titled 'Why were the BAFTAs so White?' They all quoted my tirade about the lack of Black people nominated for awards. I'd ranted about the fact that all the executive producers, directors and scriptwriters I saw picking up awards were White. I was just generally angry at the complete lack of awards for any non-White people either in front of or behind the camera. Whilst normally I would keep my feelings and opinions to myself, that night I let that poor unsuspecting journalist have it between the eyes with both barrels. Horrible.

It was weird because the next day when I woke up, I didn't remember half of what I'd said. It was just an emotional outpouring. But as I read through the newspaper pieces, one thing struck me as wrong. The *Evening Standard* quoted me as saying, 'In two hundred years' time, our children are going to look back to now and say, "Remember that really weird period when there weren't any Black people making programmes?"'

When I say it struck me as wrong, I don't mean they misquoted me. I mean I was scared it wasn't true. I was scared that in two hundred years' time there will be another pissed-off Black actor just like me (probably with more hair and better-looking), leaving another awards ceremony, complaining about exactly the same things. Our jet-pack-wearing descendants won't be saying, 'Remember that really weird period when there weren't any Black people making programmes?' They are going to be saying, 'Why didn't anyone do anything two hundred years ago, so we could actually have some Black folks making programmes now? It *is* 2213 after all!'

The more I thought about it, the more I realised that it wouldn't just be Black people saying this. In two hundred years' time, if things didn't change, disabled people would be making similar complaints. As far as I am aware not one nominee in an individual category had a visible disability. Women of all colours will be asking why there are still so few of them behind the camera. Of the forty-two winners officially listed behind the camera that I mentioned earlier only two-fifths were women, and that's only because the American HBO series *Girls* brought the numbers up.

It is not just television that has a problem. At the 2013 BAFTA Film Awards, a few months later, of the more than eighty individual nominations, again including categories from Best Leading Actor to Best Director, there were just *four* non-White nominees. And, for the record, none of them won. Again there was not one visibly disabled nominee and at that BAFTA ceremony, of the five Best Director nominations only one, Kathryn Bigelow, was female – she didn't win. The one woman who was nominated in the best screenwriter category, Lucy Alibar, was partnered with a man – she didn't win. In the Outstanding Debut by a British Writer, Director or Producer, there was only one female nominee, Jacqui Morris – again, she didn't win.

And it won't just be people of colour, disabled people and women asking these questions. Shock, horror – White men might even be saying, 'It's, like, totally *unfair* that we, like, constantly walk away with all the awards. Somebody should, like, *do* something.' (That would be a turn-up for the books, right?)

In those 2013 Film BAFTAs, on the nominee list for Best Actor, there was one of the most skilled practitioners of his generation, nominated for the lead role in the psychological thriller *The Master*. This is a White dude, who I now suspect was watching this awards ceremony with the same brewing rage, for exactly the same reasons I had had watching the TV awards.

It was a rage that only came to light seven years later. The actor I'm referring to was, of course, Joaquin Phoenix. Phoenix didn't win that night, but seven years later he finally picked up the Best Actor prize at the BAFTAs film ceremony for his role in *Joker*, and delivered one of the most memorable BAFTAs speeches ever. If there'd been a barn nearby, there'd be a plaque bearing the legend, *I was stormed by J. Phoenix*. The speech was *that* tumultuous.

The fact is, in the seven years between 2013 and 2020, no matter how often we prayed for it, there had *not* been a slow but inexorable move towards better representation. Once again, in the film awards not a single person of colour had been nominated in any of the acting categories. Phoenix called it as he saw it: 'Systemic racism'.

I watched the speech with my missus, astounded, as Phoenix articulated what far too many of us say only in private, 'We send a very clear message to people of colour that you're not welcome here.' His speech was a wake-up call for the British film and television industry and made headlines around the world. He didn't just stop at calling it 'systemic racism', he went further and said something I cheered at the time, but now conversely disagree with. He said, 'It is the obligation of the people who have created and benefit from the system of oppression to be the ones to dismantle it. So that's on us.'

He is, of course, correct that it is the duty of the people in positions of power to change a system that excludes far too many. But it is not just the obligation of one group of people to bring about change. It is the obligation of everyone. And by 'everyone', I don't mean 'other people', or 'politicians' or 'industry executives', which is what I find people usually mean when they say 'everyone'.

In 2013, seven years before Phoenix's speech, over the breakfast table I realised I had to roll up my sleeves and be part of that solution. If the dial had hardly moved in the forty years in which I had worked in television, why had I assumed that it would just miraculously move by itself in the next forty years? Or even two hundred years?

That is why a bad pun and a few newspaper articles set me on a path which would change my life for ever. I've tried to make my quote come true, that people will be saying 'Remember that really weird period when there weren't any Black people making programmes?' My dream is to make sure it happens far sooner than two hundred years' time. For there never to be a need for me to cheer on another actor making a speech about 'systemic racism'.

Now, before we get too carried away about the BAFTAs, I just want to clear up one common misconception. This is not a story about how I want more disabled, Black and working-class luvvies receiving awards and handing them out to each other. This was not an #OscarsSoWhite moment – the hashtag launched in 2015 to try to get more people of colour receiving awards. I'm not saying it is a bad campaign, but it is not what has driven me to fight for more diversity – I can't stand the word 'diversity', by the way. More on that later.

This wasn't about the glamorous winners. After all, every few years you do see a few more non-White winners, such as in the BAFTA 2020 Television Awards, which saw a few more Black and Asian people pick up gongs. This looked great, but industry insiders know that just two weeks earlier not a single Black or Asian person won a BAFTA Craft Award – the awards given to the directors, writers and people who make the programmes.

Awards ceremonies cast a light on the industry they celebrate. Whether they're for the television or film industries or an evening recognising the double-glazing or plumbing industry. Here is the secret that no one tells you: if you want to know who *really* controls the industry, take your eyes off the stage.

The stage where the awards are given out to the handful of winning nominees is merely the tip of the iceberg. The other 90 per cent of that iceberg is sitting at the tables around the stage. The power-brokers who control the industry, in this case the film industry, are literally and metaphorically in the shadows. Not in some sinister cat-stroking, secret lair in the Bermuda Triangle, James Bond villain kind of way. More in the boring civil servant type of way. The studio heads, executives and media regulators are all there at the awards ceremonies. Unlike the nominees, they are there year after year – they are people that *control* the industry.

Viewers might focus on the glittering celebrities who receive and then go home with the ugly-ass gongs, but if you want to change the industry, you can't do it by concentrating on the 10 per cent above the water in the spotlight. You do it by looking at the 90 per cent below the surface who never even leave their seats.

My pun-tastic effort did not start me on a journey to change the glossy people we see on our television screens. It set me on a quest to change the people who control the industry. That is a journey I think we can all relate to, whatever our line of work.

It is not just BAFTA and the film and television industry that has a problem. In the UK less than 7 per cent of police officers are non-White. Less than 10 per cent of British teachers are people of colour, and that drops to less than 5 per cent for head teachers. There are just six female chief executives of companies in the FTSE 100. When it comes to the country's top judges, almost two-thirds – 65 per cent – went to private school, despite the fact that only 7 per cent of the population receive a private education.

We live in a society that excludes far too many people, from far too many walks of life. It is time we focus on just one aspect of Joaquin Phoenix's speech when he said we must 'dismantle' the system, and ensure everyone can access all areas of power throughout society.

The question is: how?

It is a question I have been trying to answer for the last seven years. I want to share some of that journey with you and some of the lessons I have learnt along the way. It might have all started with a terrible pun but this is no joking matter.

(For the record, there are some very good puns on the circuit. Masai Graham, a pun fu master, won the National Pun Championships with this: 'I'm a 35-year-old mixed-race guy from West Bromwich, so I've got a reputation to uphold. It's difficult for me to write jokes about flowers, without the stigma attached . . .' Thank you, good night! Please tip your waitresses on your way out.)

2

96.9

When I first proposed that Marcus and I should collaborate on this book, the publishers invited us in for coffee and biscuits. Joaquin Phoenix had just made his speech and it seemed like it might be a good time to write something on media diversity. This was before Covid-19 had turned everything upside down and before Black Lives Matter had swept the world following the death of George Floyd. The sad reality is, I suspect, it is always a 'good time' to write this kind of book.

I arrived at Faber's offices near the British Museum with my learned colleague, marathon-runnin' Marcus Ryder, and we were ushered into a room they call Arcadia – it's at the back of the building, has a large table and is lined with lots of bookshelves. Lovely.

Waiting at that table was all-round good egg Walter Donohue, and after a few brief pleasantries about the weather and some damn fine coffee, we were joined by Alex Bowler. Walter is originally from New

Jersey, and has the kind of laid-back, world-weary persona where you feel nothing could shock him. He has seen it all before and although patient and polite, clearly doesn't suffer fools gladly. Alex is younger, and after meeting him just once, you just know that he is a bottle-rocket firework destined for greatness.

Alex exudes the kind of youthful, boisterous energy that gives the impression he's about to make his first million in the next five minutes. Walter is the older Mr Seen-It-All, who sits you down, lists the bizarre ways he spent a million in the eighties, and is now happy just to read a good book. If they ever leave the world of publishing, they would make great characters in a cop buddy movie. I just don't want to be the police chief that tells them they have to hand over their badges and they have forty-eight hours to solve the crime because the DA's on my ass . . . (I get easily distracted in business meetings.)

Anyway, they both thought it was 'good timing' for a book on diversity. After a brief while discussing the book's possible content, they asked me the sixty-four-thousand-dollar question all publishers ask a prospective author: 'Who is the target audience for this book'?

My answer was simple: 'Everyone.'

Walter and Alex looked at each other and smiled, which told me that they've heard people say this before and they just didn't believe it. They kindly explained to me, the way a patient parent explains to an excited child, that no book appeals to everyone. Not even Julia Donaldson appeals to everyone. (I love *The Gruffalo*. I want to go down to the deep dark wood. Talking mice for *life*, yo.)

And then came the line that almost felt like a physical punch in the stomach.

'This is a book about diversity, so, by definition, this is a book about a minority of people.'

I conceded that they were right, the book might not appeal to everyone – maybe that was an oversell – but it definitely wasn't about 'a minority'. Let me explain how we answered their question and subsequently further explain how that answer changes the way we should all think about diversity. It all has to do with a retired White woman who most people would not think of when talking about diversity.

Her name is Susie Symes and she is a woman on a mission. Susie loves facts and figures. More specifically, she loves to correct lazy thinking and wrong assumptions by using data and statistics. It is one of the reasons she helped to set up 19 Princelet Street

– Britain's first museum dedicated to immigration and diversity. It's in Spitalfields. A teeny-tiny museum, for Borrowers only. More people could fit into a small camper van than into this museum. You could get maybe one – at a pinch, two and a half – Ewoks in there. But for Susie its size is not the point. 19 Princelet Street has one job to do: to correct some of the incorrect assumptions about immigration.

Did Black people first arrive in the UK on HMS *Windrush* from Jamaica in 1948? No. 19 Princelet Street has all the facts and figures showing a Black presence on British shores since Roman times. Are immigrants a massive drain on the country's education and healthcare system? No. 19 Princelet Street can give you the economic data of how much immigrants pay in taxes versus how much they receive in benefits or use public services.

Susie loves her immigration stats, facts and figures. So do we. But she loves them more because she spent a large part of her working life as an economist for Her Majesty's Treasury. One of the pieces of lazy thinking she loves to squish is the idea that diversity is a *minority* issue. In fact, she says it is a majority issue. When we think about diversity, she explains, we invariably think about marginalised, disadvantaged groups. But answer these questions and see if they apply to you.

- Do you often feel excluded from society?

- Do you ever feel like you are living in the 'wrong' part of the country to really have your voice heard?

- Do you ever feel you are the 'wrong' colour to call yourself British with the same confidence as someone else?

  - Are you gay or lesbian? Are you routinely made to feel wrong because you are seen to love the 'wrong' person?

- Would you describe yourself as 'typical' or 'normal'?

- Are you simply just the 'wrong' gender to get paid equally, pursue the career you want or have an equal chance of getting the top jobs?

If you answer yes to any of these questions, according to Susie, you are in the majority. In her typical Treasury-tastic statistical way, Susie has crunched the numbers and proved that people who are counted

17

as diverse, which we think of as a minority, are, in fact, the majority. She looks at what percentage of the population are women and then combines that with the percentage of the population which is disabled, then she combines that with the percentage of the population which is non-White, then finally tops it all off by adding the percentage of the population that says they are lesbian, gay, bisexual or trans.

I am definitely not a statistician (just like I wasn't a real chef or from Brixton or a soul-singin' sex god), so I don't know how she does it, but Susie then makes sure that she doesn't do something called 'double accounting' – counting the same person twice (or even three times) because they are a woman and disabled, or Black and gay. Then she churns out the grand number: 67.5 per cent. Or, in old money, 'two-thirds'.

That's right. According to Susie Symes, the people we generally think of as the majority – White, heterosexual, able-bodied men – make up less than a *third* of the population. The rest come under the umbrella term of 'diverse'. Which is why she prefers to use the term 'majority' rather than 'minorities' when talking about diversity. In her typical statistician's way, she prefers to pick a term with a simple mathematical meaning.

When Walter and Alex told me we were writing a book for a minority of the population, I, Lenny Henry, decided to go full Susie Symes on them and say, *'Oi! Walter and Alex! No!* We're writing for the majority.'

When someone looks at you sceptically (think Scooby Doo and crew realising the monster was actually Mr Jamerson, the janitor), you begin to doubt yourself. I hate to admit it, but even though no one questioned me that day, I doubted myself. I doubted Susie Symes. Could White, able-bodied, straight men really make up less than a third of the UK population?

They seem to make up the vast majority of every important part of society. Could our politicians, judges and police be so unrepresentative? Could our television programmes have got it wrong? Susie Symes – if you are reading this, please forgive me – I had to double-check your maths. And yes, you've guessed it, the great Susie Symes (whose statistical skills I have been praising to the heavens) got it a little wrong.

I went to the very top to check the statistics. I called up Hetan Shah, at the time the executive director of the Royal Statistical Society, and said, 'All right, Hetan, chap, can you check these numbers for me? I'll buy you a Cherry B and a cheese and pickle bap next time I see you.' Hetan Shah modestly declined and, instead, put me onto the deputy director of the Office of National Statistics, the bookkeepers of the British population's data. The deputy director said they would put their best person on the case. I felt it was complete overkill just to double-check a retired Treasury official's statistics but I knew it was important.

Four weeks later I received an email from another Susie. This time Suzi Robertson, Research Officer for the Policy Evidence and Analysis Team of the Office for National Statistics. What percentage of the UK population are White, heterosexual, able-bodied men?

29.5 per cent.

Susie Symes had got it a tiny bit wrong – they are an even smaller minority than she had estimated. Just take a moment for that to sink in – and it's not a misprint. Even now, like a two-day-old rock cake, I find it hard to process. If we had a level playing field, then, for every White, able-bodied heterosexual man you see on TV, in Parliament or in any position of power, you *should* see a woman or Black person or Asian person or disabled person or gay person. Not just once, but more than twice.

Suzi from the Office of National Statistics went one step further. She knew that I am originally from

Dudley (we've got a zoo and a canal!), just outside Birmingham, and that I was looking at these statistics for television – so they decided to add one more criterion: inside London and outside London. Why? Well, the majority of British television is still made in London and the South East. People on our TV screens, whether they are reading the news or acting in a comedy, are disproportionately from London or have South East accents. People working behind the camera invariably live in London or the surrounding areas.

So when we talk about diversity, especially when it comes to television, we should consider what percentage of the population are non-White, not heterosexual, not able-bodied, not men, *and* do not live in the South East. Because these are the people who we typically think of when we think of diversity. These are the under-represented.

The number Suzi Robertson from the ONS sent me almost knocked me off my chair.

96.9 per cent.

That's right, again that is not a misprint. The people we invariably think of as the majority make up only 3.1 per cent of the population.

The numbers are almost too staggering to comprehend. For every three White, able-bodied heterosexual men with a London accent you see on TV, you should see ninety-seven people with a Birmingham or Welsh accent, or a woman, or a lesbian or gay person, or a Black or Asian person, or a disabled person, or some combination of these characteristics.

(*Editor's note: 'You know having an accent doesn't necessarily mean you live in a place?'*

Me: 'Yes, but if they really wanted a dry statistics book they would have bought An introduction to statistics. *I think they know what I mean.'*)

Three vs. ninety-seven is the reality of the UK today. This glaring fact is so obscured by the programmes on our television screens and the radio we listen to and by every politician we see that I doubt myself whenever I am sitting in a meeting with publishers and they don't even question me but simply raise an eyebrow.

The sharper thinkers amongst you may have quickly realised that even 97 per cent is wrong because I haven't started to look at religion or class or even age. Once you start to factor in these other aspects of society 3.1 per cent is a massive overestimation.

If, at every business meeting you walked in to the majority of the people were non-White, or every other television drama had a disabled person in the lead role, in many ways *that* would be a more accurate representation than what we see right now. Yet we think of the usual lack of inclusion as so normal we don't even question it.

It is this kind of thinking that Susie Symes of the museum of immigration and diversity at 19 Princelet St wants to challenge. We think of ourselves as a minority, when really we are the majority. When I give talks up and down the country, people instinctively feel this. They might not know the exact numbers – and like me they are normally shocked when they are told the precise figure – but they know something isn't quite right. They know that things are not fair.

That is why this book is for the 96.9 per cent and more.

If you are of the mind that this new drive to make society more 'diverse' does not include you, or that the quest for 'diversity' has nothing to do with you – then you, my friends, like members of the Covid-19 fan club, are in a very, *very* small minority.

Now, just like the last chapter, where I clarified that this was not an #OscarsSoWhite moment, I want to make one thing very clear. When I say diversity is about the majority this is not me saying 'All Lives

Matter' when someone says 'Black Lives Matter'. We – the 96.9 per cent – are the majority. But that doesn't mean there aren't also important differences between us as well. That is the beauty of diversity and what my colleagues and I are fighting for: for the majority to be recognised while championing what makes us uniquely different and addressing our various concerns.

Joaquin Phoenix might have given a great speech, but just like Susie Symes, he got one thing wrong.

There are many more people excluded than they first estimated. Many, many more . . .

3

QUESTION OF TRUST

A few weeks after pun-gate at the BAFTA Television Awards, a friend of mine, a TV producer named Carlton Dixon, called and told me there was a dude from the Royal Television Society who wanted to talk to me about the headlines I'd generated.

I've often spoken about the loneliness of being the only Black person on a film or television set – or in a production meeting. On the few occasions where that hasn't been the case, the other Black man in the room is usually Carlton. He and I worked on a programme about minorities in television comedy in 2019 (*Lenny Henry's Race Through Comedy*); we also made a documentary about my comedy hero, Richard Pryor, for BBC2.

Carlton, a Black man, has worked in television for over twenty years. To say he is a rarity in the industry would be an understatement.

First of all he is a (basketball-watching, Black music-loving, Tour de France-devouring, croissant-eating)

Black man. I know, just four paragraphs into Chapter 3 and I have stated that Carlton Dixon is a Black man three times. That is how rare it is for me to work with other Black people behind the camera – I find myself having to repeat it just to reassure myself that it actually happened (like seeing a unicorn or clocking Kanye West at Lidl).

The second reason Carlton stands out in the industry is that he comes from a working-class background and, heaven forbid, has proudly held on to his working-class accent. For those who don't know, television is overwhelmingly middle class. The president of the independent television company that makes *Master-Chef*, *Big Brother* and *Broadchurch* once described it as 'hideously middle class'. He then ate a quinoa wrap, drank his almond milk frappuccino and rode his Brompton bike the hell out of there.

Carlton forged his career at the BBC, an organisation where 61 per cent of the staff come from families in which the main earner had a 'higher managerial and professional job'. For those who do not speak fluent sociology gobbledegook that means 'not working class'.

According to a report by the UK's media regulator, Ofcom, approximately only half of the people

26

working in the TV industry went to 'non-selective, state schools'. Again, for those of us who don't find ourselves constantly speaking sociology-ese, that means only half of them went to 'normal' schools. The rest went to some kind of selective school, with many going to what Britain oxymoronically terms 'public' schools which, in the rest of the world, are known as eye-wateringly expensive private schools. Schools even Lord Snooty's parents couldn't afford . . .' *How much* per term? Bugger that! Son, have you heard of a place called *Grange Hill*?'

So what else makes Carlton Dixon stand out? He has a university degree but, like myself, only got it years after leaving school. Again, a complete anomaly in an industry where it is hard to swing a cat and not hit an Oxbridge graduate. He recently told me that working in the creative industries makes him feel like the product of some weird social experiment. 'A television producer? Seriously? Yeah, right, what do you *really* do?' is something he has heard more often than he cares to remember.

The other thing about Carlton is that he is one of the most cynical people I know. Working in an environment where you are constantly an outsider can do that to you. He is deeply sceptical that the media industry will ever change. He is scathing of any mention of the word 'diversity'. And he thinks watching Arsenal play is a far better way to spend your time than supposedly trying to make the world a better place.

Carlton, a joke for you: why are Arsenal nicknamed the Gunners? Because they're always saying: 'We're gunner win the cup, we're gunner win the league, etc.' (Trad. arr. Bob Monkhouse.)

So when Carlton suggested I meet the new Chair of the Royal Television Society Diversity Committee, I was both surprised and intrigued. Someone with a job title like that would normally be the last person Carlton would trust – let alone recommend I meet. It was more out of curiosity than anything else that I agreed to the meeting. When I finally met this so-called 'diversity champion' (please flip to Chapter 6 to discover why I dislike the term 'diversity' so much), I recognised him straight away. He was a Black TV executive called Marcus Ryder. I'd done some voiceover work for him on a BBC1 docusoap a few years earlier. How about that? We really do all know each other.

What Marcus wanted that day was simple enough. He wanted to put on a panel discussion about diversity in the media industry and how we can improve it. He had read my comments about BAFTA and thought I would be a good panellist.

Now. A slight detour. Dear reader, I have no idea how you spend your days, but whether you are a student, a brain surgeon or a masked vigilante, chances are you have come across the kind of panel discussion Marcus was proposing, in one shape or another: a few industry notables sit in a row on a stage; they lament something, the world's problems – from climate change to cafeteria food to whether Justin Timberlake is better alone or with NSync – that kind of thing. For the 'diversity' group, they typically lament the lack of Black people/women/LGBTQ/disabled/ (insert under-represented group here) in their specific industry and say, 'God dammit! Something must be done.' The audience applaud like crazy. Then everybody goes home.

It's like a big, velvety, group hug. Feels nice at the time but it doesn't change anything. When Marcus suggested I sit on one of these panels, I wasn't exactly enthralled. I ranted a bit about the panels being a waste of time and kept on asking him what he was hoping to achieve by putting on a panel discussion. What was the point? I've seen *Les Miserables* . . .

Those guys stormed the barricades! They didn't have a panel discussion!

In fact, I was a bit annoyed with Carlton – my normally go-to guy for no-nonsense stuff – for even suggesting I meet with Marcus. After BAFTA pun-gate, I had decided I wanted to make a real change, not just talk about it. I didn't know what I wanted to do exactly, but a diversity hug-fest was not what I was looking for.

Then Marcus said something I hadn't heard before.

He said that the panel discussion shouldn't be about how there is not enough diversity in the industry. Instead, it should be about whether we need to introduce diversity quotas into the television industry – whether a certain number of jobs should be reserved for ethnic minorities, disabled people or other under-represented groups.

Now, I'll talk about the questions Marcus was raising – quotas in particular – in a minute. But I want to finish my slight detour about panel discussions first. What I found interesting about this panel idea was that Marcus was saying we were going to be talking about solutions. Talking about their pros and cons, their rationales and challenges. Finally, we were going to talk about what we could do to make things better rather than just complain. What actually tipped the balance for me was the other Black man in the room – Carlton Dixon.

Despite having a string of reasonably successful television credits to his name, a university degree and a scintillating tango (did I mention his ballroom dancing skills?), Carlton struggles in pitch meetings when trying to sell programme ideas to television commissioners – I've seen this. Often the commissioners just don't seem to trust him. I know that sounds terrible, but in television – and I'm sure it is true for other industries – people need to trust you.

Executives need to trust your taste as to what makes a good programme; they must also approve of your editorial judgement. Every time a TV executive commissions a programme, they are giving a director or producer a large sum of money and effectively telling them to come back with a great programme. (They need to know you won't take their money and buy a classic monster truck and a crate of bourbon.)

Yes, Carlton, and every other producer who pitches a programme, has to pitch the idea to the executive, yes, executives read treatments, and, yes, there are long meetings during the course of the production process. (Long-ass meetings. So long, you have to shave halfway through. Guys, too.) All of these things are designed to mitigate risk and increase the possibility of success.

Essentially, though, any media executive eventually has to trust the person to whom they are giving the contract – irrespective of how much micro-managing they can and may want to do. The problem is, trust is such a difficult beast to pin down. (I'm talking about television here, but I'm pretty sure almost everyone can relate.)

I know I was just being scathing of sociology flap-doodle but a famous French sociologist called Pierre Bourdieu might help us understand this problem by talking about the different types of capital a person possesses. It is these different types of 'capital' that can help determine how successful you are in life. To put it simply, Bourdieu said people had several types of 'capital', not just money. For example a person has 'academic capital' (university degrees – some universities are definitely worth more than others), 'linguistic capital' (how you speak, what kind of accent you have), 'cultural capital' (the kind of films, music or even restaurants you know and like) 'symbolic capital' (various awards or titles you might have) and 'social capital' (the different networks you might have and might be able to call upon – sometimes thought of as the 'old school tie').

Bourdieu conducted surveys of the different types of music people in France liked to listen to – he was writing a little while ago, so we're not talking BTS vs. Ed Sheeran. What he found was that while manual workers liked Strauss's 'The Blue Danube', they weren't into Bach's 'The Well-Tempered Clavier', which was better suited to middle-class academics; their tastes were the opposite of their blue-collar peers.

Here is the important point of his theory: your taste in music didn't just signify whether you were part of a specific group; your taste in music dictated whether you were allowed into the group in the first place. According to his theory, the more capital you have in all its different forms, the more people trust you – and that literally translates into real money. Let television people know you went to Cambridge, instead of having a degree from another perfectly good university, and they give you the job. Walk into the room speaking with a posh accent, as opposed to one that marks you out as growing up in Dudley, and they trust you more.

It gets even more stupid. If you prefer the films and comedy that the people handing out the contracts have (the same cultural tastes), they trust you more. For a Black guy with quirky musical taste, from a working-class background, who got his degree later on in life, Carlton just doesn't have enough social, linguistic and cultural capital to get the commissioners to trust him when he walks into the pitch meetings, despite the fact that he is a great producer and has almost as many awards as sneakers (did I mention his enormous massive sneaker collection? NB a different type of cultural capital . . .).

This goes to the crux of the problem for me.

Nearly all the people I have met in television are nice and liberal. None of them are secret members of the Ku Klux Klan, nor do they go to anti-immigrant rallies on their days off. If they *did* do that, I'd see it, right? Watching *News at Ten* . . . 'Hang on, isn't that Dave stood next to the burning cross?'

Carlton heroically attempting to pitch the programme in a more intellectual way, whilst giving examples of other successful programmes he's worked on in the past, doesn't seem to cut through the basic problem of the gatekeepers' innate lack of trust. That lack of trust comes down to his social, cultural, linguistic and academic capital.

I've even seen some Black people try to circumvent

this problem by trying to 'learn' new tastes and 'improve' their capital. One time, I hitched a ride in the car of a young working-class Black researcher just embarking upon his first job at the BBC. I'm there in the passenger seat – flipping through his radio pre-sets (I know, how rude. I don't even really know this person, yet I'm passing judgement on his chosen radio stations . . .), and they were all pre-set to Black pirate radio stations (it *was* the nineties). However, by the end of the production six months later, when this dude gave me another lift, I got into his car, wanting to listen to tunes, flipped through the radio pre-sets and, get this, they had all changed to Radio 1, Radio 4, Radio London. All perfectly good radio stations, of course, but very different culturally.

It depressed me. I had no idea whether the researcher had done it consciously or not, but this told me that if you're Black and you want to survive in television, then you need to dispense with your Black working-class taste and align more with your boss's preferences. It even made me think, Well, what's the point of employing more marginalised people, if, in order to succeed, they need to align their taste with their bosses? What kind of messed-up stuff is that?

I've picked Carlton and this young researcher as examples but there is not a Black producer or woman or working-class person or disabled person I have spoken to who hasn't suffered from the same problem of not being trusted. I want to stress again that the people in power who are doing the not-trusting are *really* nice people. They are often the first to say that we need to increase diversity. But then when it comes to handing over the money, giving people jobs, *trusting* them – something gets in the way.

I can argue till I am blue in the face why TV executives should trust a Black or Brown person or someone from another ethnic group, but if deep down they don't, there's almost no point. It is trying to argue with someone about why they should fancy one person over another.

We need to find a way to cut through this problem of trust. The qualities people are judged by are unfair and often have no bearing on whether they can do the job. People like Carlton walk into a commissioner's office and the deck is already stacked against them – the playing field is nowhere near level.

That's what Marcus's panel discussion was going to be about. And it's ultimately why Carlton introduced me to him. They wanted me to discuss . . .

yes . . . *quotas* as a way to cut through this problem of trust that all three of us had experienced at different times.

Now, in many circles, 'quotas' is a dirty word. When I first heard about quotas, the idea didn't sit well with me. I was raised in Dudley – I think I've mentioned Dudley (we've gorra zoo, a castle, a canal, the Black Country Museum . . . bostin' pies) and despite my Jamaican parentage, I realise a lot of my values are very British. My mother might have cooked ackee and saltfish every Saturday morning (Jamaica's national dish) but my childhood was also filled with Ribena and saveloy and chips. I am definitely British, and quotas just seem to go against the grain of British values and the idea of a 'level playing field'.

But Marcus was *very* persuasive that day (think Kaa the python in *The Jungle Book* – that kind of persuasive). He talked to me about a whole heap of social studies; he even had a special model he wanted me to discuss on the panel (*not* Naomi Campbell). He suggested the quota idea could be modelled on the way Norway has specific laws requiring that women make up a minimum of 40 per cent of corporate boards. Back in 2001, women made up just 5 per cent of the country's directors. The government passed the law in 2005 and gave companies two years to comply. By 2008 they had reached their target.

I wondered.

Maybe?

3.5

I'M NO LEMON

When I first spoke to Marcus about writing this book, the working title was: 'Don't Blame the Victim: Lenny's Adventures in Diversity Wonderland'. Everybody I spoke to got the reference in the sub-heading to *Alice's Adventures in Wonderland*: discussions about diversity are often completely crazy. They can drive you mad; you frequently feel as if you are in a bizarre world where you are constantly in a rush but not getting anywhere.

Most people didn't immediately understand the main title, 'Don't Blame the Victim'. And titles are a bit like jokes – if you have to explain how the punchline works, you know you've failed before you've even started. (*Me on stage at Jollees Nightclub, 1976*: 'No, you don't understand. See, the dog? I gave the dog money to get the— Wait, stop talking, it's funny because I – the dog – went out, with money I had *given* him . . . (*Stops and listens momentarily.*) No, ma'am, the dog did not have a *wallet*— Agghghghgh!

I hate you all! (Storms off stage.)

The idea of not blaming the victim was key to why I originally agreed to take part in the panel discussion about quotas and, since then, it has been core to all my thinking about diversity and increasing representation in television and beyond.

Let's take a deeper dive. When I said previously that all too often people don't offer solutions for how to increase diversity, that statement is only half true. There is one solution that is often . . . no, pretty much always wheeled out. *Training.*

Take Carlton, in the last chapter, as an example. When people in powerful positions in the industry hear that Carlton might have problems successfully pitching his programme ideas, the solution they typically jump to is that maybe we need to create a diversity pitching training programme. Not enough women film and TV writers? Set up a women's diversity writers' training programme. Not enough disabled film and TV directors? Set up a diversity disabled directors' training programme. Sometimes the training is even labelled a 'leadership' programme. Not enough Black people in senior management? Set up a diversity 'BAME' senior management programme. (BAMESMP – sounds like a Wu-Tang Clan album track.)

This kneejerk response to our lack of progress – offering more training – is repeated time and time again. The big problem with all these training or leadership programmes is they implicitly, and sometimes even explicitly, suggest that the reason why women or disabled people or Black people have not progressed is because we are not capable. They are saying that what organisations and companies need to do is give the *not quite good enough* people from under-represented groups just a smidge more training to make them better. Then, and only then, will we be adequate to become executive producers, commissioners, writers, directors; to enter senior management, or fill whatever positions that currently lack diversity.

What they are doing is blaming the victim for our own lack of representation. This can often do a lot more harm than good (like eating a fourth dumpling, it seems like a good idea at the time . . .).

In the previous chapters we met Susie Symes and Carlton Dixon, so let me introduce you to another person in my cast of diverse characters and, for reasons that will become apparent, I will use a pseudonym. I met Michael several years ago, just after I'd given a talk about diversity. Over the last few years, large organisations, from the British Army to multinational banks, have asked me to make speeches about representation and inclusion. However, for me, nine times out of ten, the interesting stuff occurs after the speech, when the official questions-and-answers session is over.

It's when I'm walking to the bathroom or heading to the car that a Black person from the company approaches – when they think they're finally out of sight of their bosses. The initial part of the conversation always goes like this: 'Hi Lenny, I loved what you said in there' (a few furtive glances to triple-check no one can overhear us). Then they'll say, 'Look Len, I didn't want to say anything in front of everyone back there, but I just wanted to let you know the truth . . .'

It is in these hastily sought conversations – often in the shadows – that I learn what is really happening at an organisation behind the scenes. Frankly, I'm never sure what I'm meant to do in these situations because, beyond the speech and Q-and-A stuff, I have no further influence over the company – and the person talking to me does not want me to raise the problem with their bosses. They usually make me pinky swear. Instead, I believe that telling me is almost an act of catharsis for them – therapy, if you will, or to use less flowery language, 'a problem shared is a problem halved'.

It was in one of these snatched conversations that I met Michael. It was his story that brought home to me the abject failure and wrongheadedness of using training schemes to solve a lack of diversity and representation. Michael is a Black man who decided to apply for a diversity scheme at a company with an annual turnover of over a billion pounds a year. The scheme was meant to 'fast-track' Black, Asian and minority ethnic (BAME) employees to senior management. He was in a well-paid job already but he thought the best way to progress his career was to leave his current six-figure salary position and try to get on to this special fast-track scheme.

He told me that the day he was accepted onto this 'leadership' training scheme was one of the happiest moments of his life. 'A dream come true' was how he described it – despite the fact he was taking a pay cut. But his dream quickly revealed itself to be a nightmare. The very day he joined, he was informed by some of his new colleagues that the programme was 'rubbish'. It soon became apparent that the issues the organisation faced in promoting non-White staff already in the organisation were not going to be solved by recruiting new people and putting them through extra training. The organisation was repeating the same mistake that my colleagues and I see all the time – blaming the victim.

The training scheme lasted over a year and, at the end of it, Michael was euphemistically 'let go', saying goodbye to the whole fast-track thing, as well as that comfortable six-figure salary he had left behind. Yikes.

Why did this happen? Why don't diversity training schemes work? Are we against *all* on-the-job training? The answer to the last question is an emphatic *no*. On-the-job training is not only important, it is essential to increasing diversity. According to a report by the UK's Broadcast Equality and Training Regulator (BETR) published in 2011, there is a direct correlation between companies that invest in training and developing their staff, and all diversity measurements. In other words, those that train more *do* employ more people from ethnic minorities, women and disabled staff.

So, doesn't this contradict what I was saying earlier? No. Because the BETR was not talking about training for 'diverse people'. They were just looking at *overall training*. This is the big difference.

Now Marcus, my muse, co-writer and FaceTime buddy, loves his economic models and so this is how he explained it to me. I am not an economist (I possess no tweed jacket with leather elbow-patches. I do *not* smoke a meerschaum pipe) and so I got him to tell me in simple English, in words that normal people use. He says that to understand how a lot of training schemes work, you first have to understand the market for second-hand cars.

In 1970 a famous economist, George Akerlof, wrote a seminal paper on why brand-new cars lose their value the minute you drive them off the forecourt. When you buy a second-hand car, it is very difficult to tell if you are buying a car in good condition or a complete 'lemon'. Once off the forecourt, buyers – like you and me – assume the worst and treat every car like a 'lemon', so the price of all second-hand cars – whether a day or six years old – drops dramatically.

While Akerlof went on to win the Nobel Prize for Economics for this apparently revealing paper, part of it was not that simple. *Some* cars do hold their value better than others. That's why I drive a soft-top Bentley with white-wall diamond-encrusted tyres, complete with cocktail cabinet and Jacuzzi.

In the workplace, employers often have the same problem judging employees as a person buying a second-hand car. It is difficult to tell if you are promoting a star or investing in a 'lemon'. Appraisals and references can help, but they may be biased or just untrue. This is where training often comes in. Training not only equips an employee with new skills, it signals to the employer the quality of the person. Think of it as doing an AA check on the second-hand car before you buy it.

However, Marcus thinks that having separate diversity training schemes does not help employers really know if they are promoting a rising star or a 'lemon'. Separate diversity training schemes essentially devalue the entire process by creating a subset of candidates requiring 'remedial' attention. You've put the 'diverse' candidate in the 'lemon' group before they've even started. To continue the car analogy – you've gone and decided they belong in the Lada category without properly looking at them and then said, 'I wonder why I'm not feeling any of these cars?' 'Nuff said.

So, training = good.

Special training specifically for diverse candidates = bad.

Got it?

Now, the bigger problem is that people are not cars. Being put on a diversity training scheme and labelled a 'lemon' can have serious consequences. In our research for this book, we reached out to Michael and asked how he was doing. His reply was painful, and illustrated the human cost of these failed training programmes: 'I'm not proud to say it, but for a while I struggled with serious post-traumatic stress disorder and a massive collapse in professional confidence.'

Here was a person who, before entering the diversity training scheme, was earning a six-figure salary and after it was unemployed and felt he needed therapy. And that's the other problem with training schemes: if they are predicated on the idea that you are the problem, the people on the scheme often internalise the company's values and culture. In order to succeed, they are positively encouraged to absorb and then perpetuate the idea that they are 'lemons'. Shockingly, Michael was not the only one. On that particular scheme, the organisation in question recruited over ten 'fast-track' BAME potential management employees and then let them all go in the end. The company decided they were all, indeed, 'lemons'.

The good news is that now Michael is free of the diversity scheme, his career is back on track and is positively flourishing. He has a best-selling book and just wants to put the whole experience behind him. Hence, I can't reveal his real name. He only agreed to be discussed in this book anonymously, on the condition that I include the next bit of his response when we asked him what he thinks about training schemes now.

> I actually think they do [work]. I think they do exactly what they're intended to do, which is to create the appearance of doing something, while simultaneously doing absolutely nothing to improve diversity. It is a cruel and deeply unfunny joke. In retrospect, it dawned on me: if diversity schemes and initiatives posed so much as a hint of a threat to the status quo, there wouldn't be any. Hence, there are, of course, loads.

Now, I am only as cynical as Michael on bad days, but where I do generally agree with him is that if training schemes solved diversity and representation problems, we wouldn't be having to write this book.

And that is why Marcus and I needed to come up with solutions that do not blame the victim.

4

BE CAREFUL OF THE RHINO

Solutions, solutions, solutions. Rather than just complaining or rolling out more failing diversity schemes, I was starting to get a taste for wanting to do more. Solutions are a plan, and just like Colonel John 'Hannibal' Smith in *The A-Team*, I love it when a plan comes together.

When I began tentatively talking about diversity, what I couldn't understand was how everyone I spoke to in the industry knew the lack of Black people, women, disabled people (just add your under-represented group here) in the media industry was a real problem and yet the problem wasn't being solved. Like it was something they could live with, like E.T. in Elliot's closet, or Eve Polastri in *Killing Eve* not telling her husband that she is having an on–off relationship with a psychopath who wants to murder her.

For the record, these things are not sustainable.

Not only was this lack of representation in front of and behind the camera a real problem in terms of fairness, to me it spelled a looming disaster for the entire industry and society as a whole.

I knew already at that point that it was a problem for the industry because all the figures showed that people were simply switching off terrestrial British television programmes and watching other types of entertainment elsewhere that they felt more accurately reflected their lives. The trends were clear. Non-White people were watching more video-streaming services like Netflix and watching more online content than their White peers. So it was out with *Countryfile* and in with repeats of *The Fresh Prince of Bel-Air* – yaaaay!

This trend was not just a problem for the TV industry. It was a problem for the whole of society. Now bear with me as I get a little political and philosophical. What we see on the news determines what politicians talk about and actually do. We've seen this most obviously with President Trump and Fox News, and while that might be an extreme case, none of us are immune to the television we watch, the radio we listen to and the news we read.

But who sets the news agenda? In the UK there is not a single major news programme – from *BBC Breakfast News*, to the *Today Programme*, from

Panorama to *Dispatches* – which is led by a person of colour or a visibly disabled person. That is going to affect which stories they choose to broadcast, how those stories are reported and by whom.

It is not just news that is important. Drama impacts us on an emotional level. It enables us to walk in the shoes of another person and understand their reality in a way factual programmes do not. If we want to understand our diverse neighbours, if we want to be a society at peace with itself and not try to scapegoat one set of people for whatever reason, I believe drama is the best way to do that. If I want to discover which cutlery to use and the trials and tribulations of the upper classes and their servants a hundred years ago, I must watch *Downton Abbey*. And if I want to know what life for a regular Black British family is like then maybe I'll watch *Crimewatch* . . . Kiddin' ya.

Seriously, what would you watch if you wanted to clock the everyday life of a Black British family? Um . . . er . . . OK, I'll get back to you on that.

So we need true diversity in drama too.

We need disabled people telling their stories so we can understand the world from their perspective. Of course, women should have equal access to producing and directing so we can see the world through their eyes. And we need Black people, and other ethnic minorities, to be able to create dramas and comedies so others can feel both our joy and pain. (If that was a TV series, then Frankie Beverly and Maze's 'Joy and Pain' would be the theme tune. *Tuunnnnnne!*)

What I found so perplexing was that everyone I talked to, from powerful media moguls to politicians, agreed with me. They saw this huge disaster coming both in terms of the British television industry and the problems with democracy and society generally. I say it was perplexing because for a problem that everyone could see was coming, how come it wasn't being fixed? It was a classic 'grey rhino' problem.

A lot of business leaders, particularly in Asia, are obsessed with grey rhinos – especially after the Chinese president Xi Jinping talked about them in 2019. No. They are not worried that herds of wild elderly animals from parts of Africa will stampede across Asia on mobility scooters. 'Grey rhinos' was a term first coined by US policy analyst Michele Wucker. She uses the grey rhino as a metaphor for a problem that we know is coming – we can see the dust cloud on the horizon long before the charging animal comes into view – but all too often we don't take the necessary actions to avert the disaster until we see the actual rhino, by which time it is far too late! Your picnic is smooshed, your car is wrecked, you have a rhino horn jammed into your left glute. (Thanks for that image, Len. You're welcome.)

Even though Michele Wucker is American, the idea has really struck a chord in China with slowing economic growth, an ageing demographic and the signs of other social and economic problems that have yet to come to fruition. Here in the UK, obvious examples of grey rhinos are issues such as climate change, the state pensions' black hole and, of course, the funding of the NHS. A lot of people have even argued that Covid-19 was a grey rhino problem. We didn't know the exact details of this particular coronavirus beforehand but we could have been better prepared for a pandemic that experts had long predicted.

For me, diversity is possibly the biggest grey rhino facing British media, and the UK more broadly, because it should be part of how we approach every issue. The demography of the UK is changing. By 2031 one in five Britons will be from a Black, Asian or minority ethnic background and that number is forecast to increase to almost one-third of the population by 2061. All the research shows this growing segment of the population uses streaming services more than their White counterparts and feels that services like Netflix do a better job at representing their lives than programmes produced by broadcasters such as the BBC. Anyone who knows anything about the UK television industry, diversity and the UK's changing demographic can see the dust clouds of the charging grey rhino, horns and all.

So why are people so bad at dealing with it?

Here are a few theories. First, many grey rhinos are often created by our own existing work practices and biases. Leaders might know a possible solution, but to admit what they've been doing in the past is the problem, to acknowledge that *they* are to blame, requires them to challenge themselves and change everything that has brought them personal success so far. That is no easy exercise.

Second, politicians and executives – with their four- to five-year election cycles and golden parachutes – are far more likely to focus on the short-term, trying to muddle through and hoping to push any hard decisions on to the next person in charge. So the grey rhino doesn't smash through their living-room wall whilst they're holding the baby. (Sorry, my bad: *horrible* image. I absolutely promise not to mix metaphors in the future.)

Which brings us to the third, and possibly the most important reason people fail to deal with grey rhinos. We might know of possible solutions, but making them work is hard and fraught with danger. If leaders make the wrong decisions, they can actually make matters worse. As Michele Wucker writes: 'Choosing the wrong response to a problem can hurt a leader more than doing nothing.' Take the example of global warming: should we invest in wind, solar or wave energy, or even nuclear power? Making the wrong decision could cost a leader his or her job – while doing nothing – leaving it to a successor – might be the easier course of action.

We can see examples of all three problems in the way broadcasters have tried to deal with the oncoming diversity grey rhino.

First, for most television executives in the UK, embracing diversity has never ever made any difference to their careers. They've become successful even though television has remained incredibly un-diverse. It is hard for them to suddenly change everything that has brought them personal success so far in their lives and careers for a problem they hope is still a way off. ('Thank God that whole diversity mess didn't hit the fan. Good. Now let me die in peace and some other schmuck can deal with it.')

Second, you can see how broadcasters continue to muddle through with their same old, same old solutions. Let's bring in a new training scheme! Wait! Let's conjure up a mentoring scheme there. Or is it time for a brand-spanking-new (but same as the two dozen we've already had) leadership initiative? (Oh, don't get me started. The infantilisation of the Black, Asian and minority ethnic workforce via workshops and initiatives is the biggest pain in the butt known to humankind. We want a job commensurate to our talents and qualifications – we do *not* want to go on a course to learn something we already know and have trained for, capisce? When Idris Elba left the UK for the US, it wasn't because he'd just got on to a new training scheme – he needed a break, not an apprenticeship.)

Third, dealing with diversity requires some very hard leadership decisions. It may require adopting completely new business models more in line with Netflix and streaming services rather than the traditional broadcasting model, for example. Or it may require a completely new way of measuring success and justifying that to shareholders (in the case of ITV and Channel 5) or politicians and the public (in the case of Channel 4 and the BBC). And it will almost definitely require serious experimentation with the type of programmes broadcasters produce and the type of people who make them.

While we might understand the reasons why large organisations do not tackle massive grey rhinos, experience has shown that invariably inaction is far worse and costlier than taking action. The executives at Blockbuster video store thought it would just be too costly to move all their wonderful video tapes online; they filed for bankruptcy in 2010 almost a billion dollars in debt.

If British broadcasters don't tackle the diversity grey rhino now, they run the risk of losing large parts of their audience for ever. They risk losing money and favour. So maybe it's time for all the British broadcasters to confront the grey rhino racing towards them before its too late.

But can they?

It was a breakthrough for me when I realised that the failure to increase the number of marginalised groups in our industries was a grey rhino problem. Previous to that, I was always trying to explain the problem and why it was important. That was completely the wrong approach.

It's like trying to explain to everyone that climate change is bad and will eventually decimate not only the world's population but also the global economy. The people in positions of power across the world already know this, to Greta Thunberg and her supporters' great chagrin. Sometimes we tell them that the grey rhino of climate change is bigger or closer than they thought but they all know it is coming. (OK, *nearly* all – but I doubt President Trump is reading this book anyway. He's probably shining a torch through his veins and drinking Domestos. Bon appétit, Donald.)

What leaders want are solutions. If they are frozen in the face of a grey rhino charging towards them, it is because they don't know how to get out of the way. So, like I said earlier, I realised that if I wanted to change diversity in the media industry, I had to take a deep dive into the solutions business, not the complaining business.

The first opportunity to do just that came when an organisation called Creative Skillset published a census of diversity in the British creative industries. What they found was shocking. Between 2006 and 2012 the number of non-White people working in the industry had fallen from 7.4 per cent to just 5.4 per cent.

Things were not just standing still. They were getting worse.

Everyone in the industry was shocked, so the Minister for Culture, Ed Vaizey, convened a massive meeting of every broadcaster, trade union, TV and film person – basically a pot-pourri of the great and the good – to discuss the problem in a private chamber in the Houses of Parliament. I managed to get an invite, but was worried I was going to be thrust into another useless grey rhino event. Complaining about the coming disaster with no action actually taking place.

Look ma, the Rhino's gonna smash through the building! Let's just stand here and watch as it stampedes us all!

So with Marcus Ryder (remember him? Co-author of this book, top athlete), I hatched a plan.

We would present a solution.

We could not do this alone, so Marcus roped in one of the people who had been on the last panel discussion with me – Mr Good-lookin' himself, writer, director, producer Kwame Kwei-Armah. I have known Kwame for years and have traded a few war stories with him about being a Black guy in the industry. For those of you above the age of thirty, you might recognise Kwame from his role on the BBC's long-running medical drama, *Casualty* – he played the dashing paramedic Finlay Newton. But that was back in the day, bruv. Right now, Kwame is the Director of the Young Vic theatre – one of the most important public venues in the UK, but at the time, back in 2014, he was working in the US. He flew back (on his own dime) especially for this meeting.

The solution we were going to present was simple.

We had seen how the BBC had increased regional diversity from 9 per cent of network programmes being made outside of London to almost 50 per cent over an amazingly short period of time. The BBC had achieved this by introducing a raft of measures. The most important had been what it called 'ring-fenced money'. They had put aside a bunch of money that they said commissioners could spend *only* on programmes made outside of London. It had worked wonders.

Why reinvent the wheel? Our solution was to say, *let's do the same*. Let's ring fence money for productions that meet certain diversity criteria. And diversity criteria didn't have to be only about Black and Brown people. It could involve women and disabled people as well. If a TV production had a woman director or the script was written by a person of colour, or if half of the people employed were disabled, then it could get access to this special 'ring-fenced' pot of money – there was a lot more to the diversity criteria, but you get the general principle.

We were excited. We were going to deal with this crazy huge grey rhino using solutions that had already worked. Marcus typed up the proposal, emailed it round to a few of our friends, who tweaked it, and then we printed out about a hundred copies and headed to the meeting. I entered the room with my business partner at the time, Barbara Emile. Kwame entered a few minutes later on purpose and we sat in different parts of the room so it looked like we weren't together.

As we'd predicted, everyone went into grey rhino complaining mode: talking about the problem and the looming disaster while offering nothing but the age-old incremental tinkering solutions that had actually seen the numbers of non-White people drop.

Then Marcus and Barbara handed out the two sheets of A4 paper outlining our plan for ring-fenced money. I talked the room through it. After I finished, Kwame 'independently' stood up and talked about the positives of the plan. Just having two apparently unconnected people in different parts of the room made all the difference. You could feel people sitting up and taking it seriously.

Then something extraordinary happened. The Minister for Culture, Ed Vaizey, gave it a name. He called it the Henry Plan and the meeting attendees were soon discussing its positives and negatives. Not everyone was convinced, but the Henry Plan was now part of any possible solution. Our idea had worked. Offering a solution rather than simply reiterating the problem was the only way forward.

A few weeks later, I was asked by BAFTA to deliver a keynote speech and I jumped at the opportunity. This would be my chance to set out more details on the Henry Plan and present it to a wider audience. My experience with Kwame, Marcus and Barbara demonstrated that campaigning always worked best when you had a whole team involved, so I called up a core group of people with years of experience in the industry and together we wrote a speech setting out the problem, explaining why it needed to be solved, the solutions that had failed previously and the ring-fenced money solution we were proposing.

But we realised that it wasn't enough. So we followed it up with an open letter in the *Guardian*, signed by everyone from Richard Curtis to Meera

Syal, to all the broadcasters calling for them to implement ring-fenced funds.

In less than a year, I had somehow gone from making a silly (but pointed) joke at a BAFTA Television Awards ceremony to launching the 'Henry Plan' in the Houses of Parliament and beyond. We felt buoyed by the winds of change and pretty soon, change was gonna come. But this was no Sam Cooke record – change, if it ever did happen, was going to be a bloody and combative affair.

The powers-that-be were reluctant to alter the status quo and would only relinquish their hold either by the most persuasive argument ever put forward or by some kind of force. We were on the side of the angels, right? What could go wrong?

(Lenny keels over from exhaustion, just thinking about the long list of things that happened next . . .)

5

SCARED

After the BAFTA speech I was on an emotional high. *High?* I was like lovely Russell Brand in the bad old days – I was flying, buck nekkid, no wings – just *vroooom!*

I felt I was unstoppable. Together with Marcus and a host of other media professionals, we were creating a movement. We were finally being heard. This was not a group of disgruntled media professionals whining because they hadn't got the promotions they felt they deserved or the television series commissions they wanted. These were highly successful media professionals saying that something needed to be done and, more importantly, we were articulating what those things were. We were putting forward real solutions based on what had worked previously. We were a squad, dammit!

I then got an email out of the blue from the Houses of Parliament Culture, Media and Sport Select Committee. They were holding an inquiry into the future of the BBC and they wanted to 'examine my proposal to increase the number of Black, Asian and minority ethnic people in the television industry'.

The people who run the country – the people who decide how much money the BBC should get – wanted to hear from me. They wanted to hear my solutions, my 'proposal', for increasing diversity. I was more excited than the cast of *Love Island* on 'dress down Friday'.

So far I had been effective because I hadn't been alone. I had trusted in the wisdom of a larger group. When I had gone to the industry round table, I hadn't just gone in by myself and, even though the written proposal we had handed out was now being called the 'Henry Paper', it was only good because it was a consensus; we had gathered a group of smart people around us, and *everyone* had worked on it.

Therefore, I knew I couldn't go into Parliament and speak to the Select Committee on my own. I quickly replied to the Select Committee and told them I'd only do it if I could bring two people: Pat Younge, the former head of BBC Television Production – at that point the highest position ever reached by a Black person at the BBC; and Marcus Ryder, who was rapidly becoming my consigliere, my Tom Hagen. (We weren't gonna have anybody whacked, but it's always good to have an adviser like this – juuust in case . . .)

The Committee agreed and the date was set for 24 June 2014. Pat, Marcus and I agreed to meet a few days before to prepare what we would say. We also role-played – trying to anticipate the questions and how we would answer them.

At the time, I was trying to work through a possible one-man show on the life of Richard Pryor – my day job, as it were – and the National Theatre in London had given me studio space to write and rehearse. (The idea of a solo show based on Richard Pryor is a lifelong passion of mine, which unfortunately for the moment has been sidelined.) During one of my workshop rehearsals, the three of us met, fuelled by coffee, croissants and chocolate raisins, and worked through our game plan for about two hours – then Marcus and Pat left me to struggle through the complicated life of one of the greatest and most complex comedians who ever lived. On the face of it, the meeting went well but I could see Marcus wasn't happy. It wasn't until years later that I found out what was troubling him.

He was scared.

That sounds so obvious that you might wonder why I am even writing about it. Going in front of a Select Committee is an incredibly scary prospect, right? We all get stage fright to a lesser and greater degree, so it should not be a surprise that one of us was nervous. But this was more than just being nervous. This was real fear. Once again it illustrates an issue in trying to increase diversity both in the media and through all walks of life.

Of the three of us, Marcus was the only one who was at the time directly employed by a British broadcaster, specifically, the BBC. In many ways, he was the embodiment of the diversity we were fighting for: a Black person in a senior position behind the camera. But the day before he met Pat and me at the National Theatre studios, he had been called into a meeting with another senior BBC executive who wanted to have a 'friendly chat'. What about? The Select Committee to which we were going to give evidence. The executive told Marcus the BBC wanted to give him any 'help he might need' and offered to give him some pointers on 'what to expect'.

According to Marcus, the senior executive was true to their word. They talked about who the different politicians on the Committee would be and what they thought their respective positions were with regards to the BBC. The irony was that rather than comforting Marcus, this walk-through terrified him. While he listened to the advice of the BBC senior executive, all Marcus could think about was the fact that if we wanted real change, we would have to speak truth to power.

Over the last twenty years, diversity in the BBC and across the creative industries had arguably gone down. Collectively, we had already said that we were no longer just going to moan about how bad things were as if the current situation was caused by an act of God. But *not* doing that meant identifying what people far more powerful than us were doing wrong.

And that was scary for Marcus. He would need to tell a group of politicians very publicly what his bosses were doing wrong. I wish he'd told me about this at the time; I would have given him pen and paper so he could start drafting his resignation letter. I remember going to a session at the BBC where Marcus and I had written a speech about the lack of diversity within the organisation – I was stopped on the way out by a Black member of staff who congratulated me on my speech but told me that he couldn't publicly support what I'd said because 'I have to work here'.

Marcus was in a similar position – about to criticise his bosses and then offer solutions that many of those senior BBC figures might not want to hear. That's why he was scared. After the Select Committee was over, he would need to return to his office and say to those same powerful BBC figures: 'Hi, guys! It's Marcus here, the bloke that was saying all that stuff; can I have a promotion now? Also, can you make sure my career is *not* sidelined? Thanks. Hugs all round. *Such fun.*'

Frankly, he was worried that his career would not only be sidelined, but totally annihilated. Imagine a moon-sized flaming comet about to hit the earth – aimed at Marcus's face. That's how frightened he was. But why?

It is scary for any of us to speak uncomfortable truth to our bosses. For people from diverse backgrounds – women, disabled people, Black and Asian people – it is particularly difficult. Study after study has shown that women and people of colour pay a huge price for promoting diversity. Marcus has done a ton of academic research on this very subject.

A seminal paper titled 'Female Tokens in High-prestige Work Groups: Catalysts or Inhibitors of Group Diversification?' studied three hundred executives, both male and female. They found that when men promoted diversity, they received slightly higher performance ratings. They were perceived as 'good guys' creating a better workplace. However, when women executives promoted diversity, they were perceived as nepotistic – trying to 'advantage their own group' and their performance was then negatively perceived accordingly. In another study, by the *Harvard Business Review*, researchers found a similar result: 'Women and non-White executives who advocated for diversity were rated much worse by their bosses.' Over the last few years, Marcus has become a really good friend to me and he loves telling me about all these different academic papers, which is why I can talk about them now. But, instinctively, everybody who is perceived as coming from an under-represented group knows these kinds of results to be true.

The study that really struck fear into Marcus was one titled 'Race and Self-Presentation in the Labor Market'. It pointed to even more far-reaching implications than simply annoying his bosses at the BBC. In that study, non-White people who had previously demonstrated a tendency to advocate for diversity were shown to be less likely to be promoted or get a new job. In the study, non-White job applicants who included experiences related to their ethnicity on their CVs were more likely to be passed over for jobs – even at companies that openly valued diversity.

Marcus was terrified when he came out of that meeting with the senior BBC executive not because the executive had said anything threatening to him but because that was the moment he realised that the BBC and the broadcasting industry were actually watching and listening to what he said. He would be the Black guy who publicly 'advocated for diversity', which all the studies said would harm his career. In his head, Marcus was now picturing this as the moment when he strips off and walks into the ocean holding a large anvil. Not a good time.

In recent years, we have seen that as a non-White person, or a woman, or heaven forfend, both(!), sometimes you don't even have to openly advocate for diversity but just talk about your experience as a non-White person for it to be counted against you.

On 25 September 2019, the BBC's executive complaints unit officially found that BBC Breakfast's news presenter of colour Naga Munchetty had breached the corporation's guidelines by offering a personal opinion on President Donald Trump's comment that four congresswomen of colour, who were American citizens, should 'go back' to the 'places from which they came'. Naga openly, on camera, said the tweet was racist. Assuming not many Trump supporters are going to read this book (how could they, there're no pictures to colour in?), even I think the vast majority of people reading this book right now would agree with me that that particular Trump tweet *was* racist (just like his claims that drinking detergent might cure Covid-19 were *insane* . . . but let's just leave that there).

Anyway, Naga then said, 'Every time I have been told, as a woman of colour, to go back to where I came from, that was embedded in racism'. (As a Black man who grew up in the UK, I can vouch that this is true.) When asked by her co-presenter how this made her feel, she said: 'Furious. Absolutely furious. And I imagine lots of people in this country will be feeling absolutely furious that a man in that position thinks it's OK to skirt the lines with using language like that.' Again, that is true. For speaking her truth as a woman of colour, rather than encouraging her to continue to share her truths, the BBC's complaint unit found she had broken their editorial guidelines around 'objectivity'. Stating simple facts and relating them to her own experience were a subject of discipline.

I am not an expert in BBC editorial policy, but what

I do know is this: a woman of colour calling a racist tweet racist and telling the world how she has experienced racism should be applauded, not chastised. Imagine a person in a wheelchair being criticised for talking about their experiences of ableism. Or a trans person talking about discrimination around their gender. Or Piers Morgan being attacked for saying how upset he gets whenever he sees a vegan sausage roll. (He gets really upset; his face goes full Belisha beacon . . . it's not a pretty sight.) This was and is Naga's lived experience and she is allowed to give it a voice. Just like any other person of colour – whether it's me or Nish Kumar or Diane Abbott or Justin Trudeau when *he* was black at university.

After a public uproar, the BBC at first doubled down on its position. BBC senior executives went on television to explain why it was right to punish the Asian presenter. It wasn't until it came out that people initially complained about Naga's White male co-presenter as well as Naga, yet the complaint was dropped against him but upheld against Naga, that things changed. When the Director General of the BBC finally came out and over-ruled his entire executive committee, the disciplinary action against Naga was dropped.

When you look at this incident and how an Asian woman ended up in hot water while the White male presenter was unscathed, you realise why people can be so scared to speak their truth about diversity – let alone advocate for it. And that was precisely why I could sense something was wrong with Marcus when he left the preparatory meeting with Pat and me at the rehearsal room that day.

Soon, 24 June rolled round. Marcus, Pat and I met at the committee room and gave our evidence about the 'Henry Plan' and how we wanted money to be ring-fenced specifically for diverse productions, in a similar way to how money is ring-fenced for local and regional productions. We slipped in one more requirement: we wanted diversity to be written explicitly into the BBC Charter.

Now, the BBC Charter is basically *the* document that sets out and decides how the BBC should be run. Since the BBC is a public entity – it is funded by our licence fees, after all – the Charter is actually written by the government and updated every ten years. Pat, Marcus and I felt that putting diversity into the Charter would be a key step to ensuring that representing marginalised groups would no longer be an afterthought but would be core to how the BBC ran.

Even if I say so myself, the three of us were on fire that day.

A few weeks later, the same Select Committee summoned a group of BBC executives and asked them if they were going to implement the 'Henry Plan'. I think it's best if I transcribe exactly how they responded:

Ben Bradshaw, MP: Lenny Henry was very critical of the current schemes and initiatives and mentoring and all of this stuff. He said the only thing that will work is a similar system to the one you have on regional content. Why don't you just adopt his ideas?

Lord Hall of Birkenhead (BBC Director General Tony Hall): We have another idea, which is a pot of money for developing programmes that maybe Danny can explain.

Danny Cohen (BBC Director of Television): Lenny talked about ring fencing and what he wanted was ring fencing of production. What we propose is ring fencing development spend, because the point around getting the best ideas and a meritocracy means you guarantee that when commissioners commission ideas they are commissioning the very best wherever they have come from. So we are ring fencing around 15 per cent of our development spend, proportionate to that part of the population, for those communities to make sure that we are getting the ideas from them.

For non-TV types, let me explain how the BBC's Danny Cohen actually responded to our idea in plain English. When you pitch programme ideas to broadcasters, your ideas can often just be presented as several hundred words on two or three sheets of paper, with illustrations. Once you've jumped through a few hoops (if you're lucky) the broadcaster will commission the programme on the strength of the written proposal and the meeting, but often it is just the start of a longer process. What they sometimes do is give you development money to see if the idea is any good – run it up the flagpole, see if anyone salutes, kinda thing. Getting your hands on development money is often the first hurdle to finally getting a programme made.

What Danny was proposing was making sure that a certain amount of that money went to diverse productions. In theory, this should mean a lot more diverse productions on our screens.

Now, I was watching the Select Committee streamed live on my computer and almost spat out my tea when I heard Danny say this. A year into our campaign and we were winning! Amazing! I did the 'winning' dance around my kitchen table (it involves complicated step ball changes and fleckerls – if Craig Revel Horwood saw me doing my 'winning' dance he'd say it was *'fab-u-lous*, darling!').

At the same time it wasn't *exactly* what we were asking for. We wanted the BBC to ring fence proper money for diverse productions in the same way they ring fence proper money for regional productions – not just for development. Development money is a little less than 0.5 per cent of the BBC's overall production budget. But this was a start! I wasn't going to let the perfect be the enemy of the good.

This was good. We had shifted the debate from one where people from diverse backgrounds were complaining to one of offering solutions, and the BBC were taking on board our solutions – albeit with a twist. Then, a few months later, the government took on board our other recommendation and explicitly wrote in diversity as a core priority in the BBC Charter.

We had won! We had got everything we had asked for. The world seemed a little sunnier. I did the winning dance around the kitchen table – Craig texted 'Fbls dlng.' I knew what he meant. I was happy. Yet for some reason Marcus and Pat were only popping the Cava and not the Champagne. I was soon to find out why. But more on that later.

I know I've left something hanging. I'm sure you're wondering how Marcus overcame the fears that many under-represented people feel when he spoke at the Select Committee. How did he get 'on fire', as I put it earlier?

Now, remember, at the time he didn't even tell me that he was scared; it was just a vibe I was getting from him. It was only recently that he told me the story. After his meeting with Pat and me preparing for the select committee, he went back to his office in Glasgow as the head of BBC Scotland Current Affairs. A senior executive at BBC Scotland knew he had met with other BBC executives in London for this 'friendly chat' to brief him about the Committee. The senior White male Scottish executive came over to ask him how it went and after a very superficial conversation fixed him with a stare and simply said, 'Don't worry, go get them.'

Marcus said, on the face of it, for anyone watching the conversation, the positive affirmation would seem as meaningless as the rest of the conversation. But the words resonated with Marcus deeply. He was being told he had support in Scotland. He had an ally.

While I quoted all those studies about how speaking out about diversity can damage the careers of non-White people and women, there is a more positive way to interpret the studies. For White men, championing diversity can be *beneficial* for their careers. What Marcus and all people from under-represented groups need are *allies* to support them. And that is what the White Scottish man did for Marcus that day. He gave Marcus the strength to speak his truth – like getting a pat on the back from Braveheart: *freedom!*

If we want to create a culture where people are not scared to speak their truth, we need to create a culture of allies. If you are a Black man, you need to support your female co-worker when she is calling out sexism. If you are a White woman, support your Black co-worker when they are advocating policies to combat ethnicity pay gaps. And White men, well, you guys just have to support everyone!

One White man's words of encouragement changed how Marcus approached the Select Committee and helped change how the BBC and government approached diversity. That's how much that support can matter. Imagine if a whole group of White men got behind this? We'd be unstoppable to the nth degree. But things like that don't just fall into your lap – they have to be earned. How to convince more people to get behind us and do the diversity conga?

Dig what happened next . . .

6

NUMBERS VS. REAL LIVES

Now, before I go into why our historic victory wasn't quite everything we had hoped it would be (no solid-gold carriage clock, no Nando's black card, no bankroll of fifty-pound notes that would choke a horse – this whole thing hasn't paid off at all . . .), despite that, I want us to enjoy the moment – for one chapter at least.

I want to go into a bit more detail as to why I have become so passionately involved in the struggle for better representation of every kinda people in the media – and throughout society.

My problem with so many of the discussions around these kinds of 'diversity' issues is they often just get reduced to numbers. Why are only 14 per cent of British films directed by women when women make up over 50 per cent of film school graduates? Why are roughly only 1 per cent of directors on *EastEnders* non-White when the popular soap is set and filmed in London, which has a Black, Asian and minority ethnic population of 40 per cent? I am not saying that these statistics are not important, but if we concentrate only on the numbers, we miss something really important: the human stories behind the statistics.

I am not fighting for numbers. Abstract ideas can't motivate me to get out of bed. The fight has to be for and about real people.

This point was brought home to me when I asked Marcus, who is an obsessive marathon-runner, what he actually thinks about during the three-plus hours when he is running a marathon. His answer not only surprised me, but encouraged me and put fire in my belly as to why we need to keep fighting for diversity and never think of it as just a question of increasing numbers.

The majority of this book is written by the two of us, but I'll let Marcus explain in his own words what he said to me.

What Marcus Ryder thinks about when he runs marathons:

When I run marathons, I think about Jay Merriman-Mukoro. He was a friend and colleague.

In 2014 I qualified to run in the Boston marathon. It is one of the biggest marathons in the world and most importantly you can only qualify to run in it if you have run a special qualifying time. For that reason even just getting in is seen as the pinnacle of many amateur runners' 'careers'. That is definitely how I viewed it when I qualified to run it.

Now a few times in life something happens that puts everything in perspective. An event so dramatic that it shocks the system and either forces you to re-evaluate your beliefs or spurs you on to redouble your efforts.

The morning before I was going to run the Boston marathon I was sleeping on a friend's bed in Boston when my phone started ringing at 3.50 in the morning. At the time I was an executive producer working for BBC Scotland and it was my production manager ringing. I knew instantly something was wrong. Back in the UK it was still only ten to nine – the working day had hardly started.

'There's no easy way to say it, so I'm just going to say it,' was all the warning I got by way of preamble. 'We think Jay is dead – drowned in Barbados.' Just remembering the conversation still makes my lip quiver. Jay, my colleague, had been in Barbados for a friend's wedding, but he was also directing a film for me about the 1986 Commonwealth Games. One of the interviewees happened to live in Barbados and so, the day before, he had shot an interview with him. Work done, the following day he had gone back to enjoying his holiday. My understanding is that he swam out to sea and simply never returned.

There are supposedly seven stages to grief and I think I have gone through them all, but if I think too much about it I am quickly transported back to stage number three: anger.

Jay was a brilliant assistant producer. He had worked on numerous high-profile landmark current affairs films. Everything from The History of Modern Britain with Andrew Marr to Mixed Britannia. But like hundreds of Black people working in television before him, he felt he had hit a glass ceiling. For people who do not know the different career stages in the television industry, an assistant producer is usually just below a director. But no one would give him the break he needed to direct his first film.

I've lost count of the conversations we would have at numerous cafes in and around the BBC where we would discuss the problems of the glass ceiling. Part career advice, part therapy session, they were fundamentally just two Black people discussing the obstacles we faced. No matter how difficult the issues were, Jay would always be laughing and smiling. Everyone I spoke to who worked with him all said the same things: 'Jay is brilliant,' 'He should be directing,' 'He deserves a break.' In 2014, I was finally in a position to give him that break. BBC Scotland – due to Glasgow hosting the Commonwealth Games and the independence referendum – had more opportunities than usual.

I didn't give him the break as an act of goodwill. I gave him the break because I knew he was perfect for the job. The film was a fascinating story of an African-led boycott of the 1986 Commonwealth Games due to South African apartheid. Jay had a great track record in historical documentaries, understood how to distil complex race issues (in this case, apartheid) to a mass audience, and had brilliant visual ideas.

He had to move up to Glasgow to direct the film but he didn't hesitate. The first month he moved into the spare bedroom in my family's home while he looked for a place to stay. That's when I'd like to say the professional relationship became a friendship. I discovered he loved Radiohead; he told me how he had proposed to his wife Olivia, and about his relationship with his Nigerian father.

It is trite when someone young dies suddenly to talk about 'what a loss it is', 'a waste of talent' or 'how we lost him in his prime'. With Jay, these oft-quoted phrases have an added edge that fills me with anger and sorrow. Jay may have been finally directing his first broadcast film but there was no way this should have been his directing debut. His talent was so immense and obvious, not just to me but to everyone. He should have had a plethora of directing credits. I shouldn't have been 'giving him a break'. He should have been 'doing me a favour', directing a film I would executive produce.

We often talk about diversity in the abstract or express in numbers the lack of women, Black or disabled directors. Jay's death exposes the cruel reality behind such unemotional, cold statistics. Behind each number are countless stories about wasted talent. It is about people being held back despite amazing talent. It is about the fact that for far too many Black people working in the media, fundamentally, life is unfair. Jay's tragic and untimely *death just brings that into focus.*

Jay was never able to fulfil his potential. The same is true for too many people from diverse backgrounds working in television – we may not die as tragically and early as Jay but our untapped potential follows us to the end of our careers.

I have run more than a dozen marathons since Jay's death, on every continent in the world except Antarctica. But because of the timing of that fateful phone call, just a few hours before the Boston marathon, I find myself thinking about him during every marathon I've participated in since.

Jay inspires me when I am running, and the righteous indignation I feel when I think about his loss inspires me when I work on diversity issues.

•

We might not all have such dramatic stories to tell, but we all know what wasted talent feels like. While I ardently try to avoid the stereotype of 'angry Black dude', I'd be lying if I didn't admit to sometimes feeling anger when I think about the unfair treatment and lack of representation of marginalised people in the media industry.

Behind every boring, cold, diversity statistic there are thousands of real people whose lives are affected.

When we have a statistic such as 'less than 25 per cent of British TV programmes are directed by women', what we are really saying is: there are over a thousand individual women who have not met their potential, who have hit the glass ceiling or will never be able to pursue the careers they wanted to pursue. Women who hit the glass ceiling in their careers are more likely to suffer depression and other forms of mental health problems. Being made redundant or not being able to find a job similarly affects people's lives, without even going into the financial instability and lack of confidence it can cause.

Obviously, it is not just women – we're also talking about an immense multitude of people whose lives have been worsened due to the unfair treatment and lack of diversity they face as an under-represented group. When we talk to certain, well-meaning people in the industry, the constant refrain is, 'We're with you all the way. You're pushing against an open door.' It's maybe only when we reach the pavement outside that we think to ourselves, Hang on, if the door's open, what are we pushing against?

A few years ago, the broadcaster and journalist

Henry Bonsu appeared on the BBC Radio current affairs debate programme *Any Questions?* During the course of the programme, one thing Henry said stuck in my mind: 'Unfulfilled ambitions are the biggest cause of mental illness for Black people.' If Henry's point is true, then it could have important consequences for people from under-represented groups in general and those of us working in the media specifically.

Black British people are vastly over-represented in mental health statistics. For example, Black men are three times more likely to be admitted to British psychiatric hospitals than their White contemporaries. It would be far too simplistic to attribute all of this to diversity issues, but it would also be naïve to think this doesn't play some role.

So let me hit you with another piece of science: the gap between where a person is in society and where they think they should be has been recognised by the medical profession and is termed 'self-discrepancy'. It is this gap that can seriously affect our mental health. According to self-discrepancy theory, prejudice in the media industry could be literally making people from diverse backgrounds mentally ill. Especially as this prejudice is nearly always indirect rather than overtly in your face.

A study by Columbia University Mailman School of Public Health's Department of Epidemiology revealed that women who suffer from a gender pay gap are 2.5 times more likely to suffer from depression. So either women accept that they are worth less than men – or they recognise they are not where they should be in their careers, which means they suffer from this 'self-discrepancy' problem. Another study by Cornell University's College of Human Ecology in 2017 showed a clear link between being the victim of racial discrimination at work and a range of mental health issues.

One of the reasons Marcus himself runs is that as a Black man working in the media industry, it helps his mental health. In one form or another, if we are honest, almost every person from an under-represented group is affected, and we all have to find coping strategies. Marcus runs. I do yoga. There is also another proven way to cope with these stresses: talking.

We can lessen the effects of rejection, racism, ableism, sexism and other forms of prejudice by talking about them. Simply talking to friends about the problems we are facing, about the rejection we are suffering, and sharing common experiences, has been shown to help mental health in study after study.

The other useful thing about discussing our experiences – or writing a book – is that you turn faceless numbers into real lives. And, after all, that is what we are fighting for: real people's lives.

7

GIRL, YOU KNOW IT'S TRUE; DIVERSITY, I LOVE YOU

When something comes too easily, you need to be suspicious. Your food arrives piping hot too quick at the so-called posh restaurant? (I'm thinking *microwave*? Canned goods? Deliveroo? Did somebody say Jus' Eat?)

People have been fighting to increase diversity in the media industry and across society for decades. Yet in just over a year, with a group of friends and media professionals, my colleagues and I had been able to change the media landscape and get almost everything we asked for.

I should have been more suspicious. It was far too early to celebrate. In tennis they call this particular moment 'celebrating the point before you make the shot and earn the point' . . . Doh! The problem was that although I had worked in television since I was sixteen, I hadn't really paid too much attention to the byzantine and labyrinthine ways in which the industry functions. So, in many ways, I was still on a steep learning curve.

To comprehend the next bit of the story, you need to know a little bit about how the BBC and the BBC Charter works – don't worry, I'll make it simple because I didn't really understand the ins and outs at first. (Typical me – 'So I twirl the pasta around the fork and *then* stick it into my face? Wait, what? In my mouth? That's *genius*!)

Here goes . . .

The government assembles and writes the BBC Charter – like the Avengers meeting up at Stark Tower for a strategy meeting except without the weird costumes. The Charter is chock full of big ambitious and sweeping statements, saying the BBC should do things like 'support learning for people of all ages' and 'provide high-quality output in many different genres' and, particularly relevant in our case, 'reflect, represent and serve the diverse communities of all of the United Kingdom's nations'.

But because the BBC is independent, the government can't order them directly to meet the utopian goals laid out in the Charter. So you have another semi-independent body called Ofcom. Ofcom is the regulator for telecommunications services in the UK that, in their words, makes 'sure people get the best from their broadband, home phone and mobile services, as well as keeping an eye on TV and radio'. In terms of the Charter, it is Ofcom's job to negotiate with the BBC about the practical side of what the broadcaster needs to do to meet these goals. For example: 'The BBC should provide high-quality output in many different genres.' This means playing a certain amount of news and current affairs in prime time – the exact amount of which is what Ofcom and the BBC thrash out round the table. Or the statement, 'support learning for people of all ages' means Ofcom telling the BBC how much it needs to spend on educational programmes, along with other issues.

The government sets lofty goals; Ofcom gets its hands dirty telling the BBC what they need to do to meet those goals. Getting something written into the Charter is in fact only half the battle. The next part is how Ofcom will enforce it.

I was doing my little victory dance when I'd only completed half the race. (*Len, you damn fool! You celebratin' the basket before you even made the jump shot. Now you all sprawled out across the front row wid your broke-ass teeth . . .*)

What we needed to know was: how was Ofcom going to ensure that the BBC would actually 'reflect, represent and serve the diverse communities of all of the United Kingdom's nations'? What would that mean in reality for women and disabled people and Black people like myself?

After the Charter came out with diversity written into it, Ofcom held a consultation process on how the BBC's performance should be measured on all the things mentioned in the Charter. This consultation also included how the BBC should meet its diversity commitments. Although we should always remember the real lives behind the statistics (if you don't know that, you are clearly skipping chapters. Go directly to Chapter 6. Do not pass Chapter 8. Do not collect £200. Get an Uber now and drive back to Chapter 6 . . .), often statistics, data and the appropriate research is the only way of measuring progress.

After the initial consultation process, Ofcom tentatively said it would only set the BBC targets for *on-screen* diversity but would not set any targets for behind the camera. Now, you might think it doesn't matter who the people are working behind the camera – surely it's the people you see *on* the screen who are important. For me, that is fake diversity.

Let me explain – I know there's a lot of explaining in this chapter but this is an important point. It involves an act of imagination, a visualisation, if you will. Imagine if this book had not been written by me and Marcus, and we had merely put our names on the cover and, instead, the text had been generated by a writer who wasn't from a diverse background. We would be giving the *appearance* of diversity. But the thoughts, words, feelings and values contained within the text would not truly be from an under-represented perspective. Like I said, fake diversity.

We see examples of this in almost every industry – not just film and television. People from under-represented groups are sometimes literally rounded up to appear in company brochures to give the appearance of diversity when nothing is really changing in the corridors of power. We have all seen those corporate pictures of happy-go-lucky multicultural groups working together. Coincidently, the gender mix always seems to be 50 per cent and there is usually someone in a wheelchair smiling. Yet when we get to the office itself nearly all the Black people are serving the food and there's a set of mountainous stairs that would definitely wipe the smile from the face of any wheelchair-bound employee.

In 2019, a Google employee even accused the company of wanting to give the impression it 'cares about diversity' by tricking minority workers into accepting positions at the company by pretending jobs were more senior and interesting than they actually were. A practice that on the surface level would effectively swell their diversity stats. More recently, *GQ* was exposed for photoshopping two women into a photo of fifteen mostly White tech CEOs to make it look more diverse. How tricky is that? That's trickier than David Blaine trying to pick David Copperfield's pocket whilst watching Tommy Cooper pull two rabbits from Penn and Teller's back pockets. *That's* how tricky that is . . .

It is for these reasons that I am very mindful of just monitoring surface diversity. When it comes to actors and presenters, it is important, but superficial. Diversity behind the camera, for me, is what counts. Telling our own stories from our unique perspectives is what I believe diversity is about. That is authentic diversity.

Yet Ofcom would only set the BBC targets for on-screen diversity. It would *not* set any targets for behind the camera. The full impact of what Ofcom were actually saying took some time to sink in, but the more I thought about it, the more I felt Ofcom were saying that Black people and other under-represented groups' views and identities did not matter. Ofcom were saying that as long as we had a Black person on the TV screen acting out the words, giving the *appearance* of diversity, then it was absolutely OK even if a straight, able-bodied, Oxbridge-educated White man living in London (one of the 3 per cent – remember Chapter 2?) had written every word and directed every scene. As long as it 'felt' as if it was coming from an under-represented group, they were going to say it was diverse.

Now I love Ofcom, some of my best friends work for them, and talking to some of them privately many thought behind the camera was just as important as on-screen. But even best friends can disagree – and the fact of the matter is *what gets measured gets done*. Where the regulator sets targets – broadcasters will meet them. And Ofcom were not setting targets for behind-camera diversity.

Now this is me talking from my perspective as a Black person working in the industry. But everything I say can be applied to a greater or lesser extent to other groups. So what exactly were the numbers of non-White people working behind the camera at the BBC at the time? The BBC had just released official statistics that said 14.5 per cent of its workforce was non-White. Which is pretty impressive. Well, it is until you actually start to look at that number more closely.

A large number of those non-White staff work in the business and finance departments. They are important but they have *no influence on what programmes are being made*. The figure also includes a lot of people who work for departments like the Swahili or Arab services based in Africa and Asia, as well as specialised teams based in London often not broadcasting in English and definitely not catering to a British audience. If you take out just these two groups of people only around 9 per cent of the workforce making programmes that you and I watch are non-White.

It gets worse. That 9 per cent only includes people with BBC contracts. Over half of programmes that you watch on the BBC are made by independent companies. The BBC doesn't keep statistics on the diversity of the companies that make programmes for them. So what was the true number of non-White people working for British broadcasters and making programmes? No one knew back in 2014. But there were clues.

Every year the Royal Television Society holds Craft Awards. These are awards given to the people who work behind the camera in categories like best director, best sound recordist or best editor in various genres. In a very unscientific study, I looked up every single nominee – now, you can't tell everyone's ethnicity just by looking at their picture and profile online, but the number of non-White nominees definitely wasn't close to 9 per cent by any stretch of the imagination. For me, looking at all those pictures was like watching a *Downton Abbey* Christmas special.

There were also other clues as to how racially un-diverse things were behind the camera. Coincidentally, that same year a trade body called Directors UK, who represent TV and film directors in the UK, had published a report on how many directors at the major broadcasters were people of colour. The number that kept coming up in their report was fat and round. (No offence meant.)

In the Directors UK's sample study, the number of talk shows directed by non-White people was zero.

The number of period dramas directed by non-White people: zero.

The number of game shows directed by non-White people: zero.

The number of sketch shows directed by non-White people: zero.

The number of reality TV programmes directed by non-White people: zero.

The number of panel shows directed by non-White people: zero.

The number of children's comedy shows directed by non-White people: zero.

The number of children's entertainment shows directed by non-White people: zero.

And the number of multi-camera and entertainment shows directed by non-White people was zero. (Marcus Ryder slides me a note: 'That's not true, it was actually 0.06 per cent' – that's what I love about Marcus, always a stickler for detail.)

Not only were the numbers looking particularly bad for directors, just the year before the BBC had lost a number of its key, most influential non-White staff: Aaqil Ahmed, the first Muslim head of BBC Religion; Maxine Watson, acting head of documentary commissioning; Tamara Howe, controller of business, comedy and entertainment; and David Okuefuna, the first Black channel executive of BBC4 *and* BBC2. The Diversity Beatles have left the building!

So with Ofcom saying it would only measure on-screen diversity, I knew that the chances of diversity behind the camera being addressed were no more likely than before we had got it written into the Charter. Something needed to be done.

The first thing I did was draft a letter to Ofcom explaining why I thought they had made a mistake.

Dear Sir/Madam,

I would just like to inform you that Milli Vanilli were not a good example of diversity. I do not believe they were singing their own songs.

In fact, I don't think they wrote them either.

I did not campaign this hard for 'Milli Vanilli diversity'.

Yours sincerely,

Sir Lenny Henry

PS I also think the bloke that plays Paddington in the movies stole a real bear's only gig for that year. Disgraceful.

I looked at this for a while, took a deep breath, tore it up and regrouped my A-team colleagues who had helped me shape the 'Henry Plan', my BAFTA speech, my open letter to the broadcasters asking for ring-fenced funds, etc., and together we wrote something a little more professional.

I knew that would not be enough. I was still at the early stage of my learning curve. Nevertheless, I was beginning to understand the importance of politics in this diversity game. I enlisted the help of two other groups who campaign for media diversity: the TV Collective, run by an absolute firebrand of a woman called Simone Pennant, and another group called Act For Change. Together, in 2017, we were able to get the MP Dawn Butler to hold an event in Parliament and for me to talk about the issue of fake diversity and how Ofcom had to change its mind.

It was a powerful moment. We put the call out and told as many people as possible to come to Parliament. We had people from all different backgrounds filing into Portcullis House and making their way past centuries of history and into one of the conference rooms. To see that many people of different ethnicities, women and disabled people lifted my spirits and I gave the best speech I could give.

I included a church-style call-and-response section in the speech about the zero non-White directors in each genre and, every time I asked the room how many non-White directors there were, the congregation would shout back, 'Zero!' By the time we got to the last zero, people were literally screaming at the top of their voices. I even led everyone through a verse of 'Girl You Know It's True' by Milli Vanilli (or *was* it by Milli Vanilli? – that was the whole point, of course!).

I wanted us to be loud and brash at the epicentre of British politics so Ofcom couldn't ignore us and all the politicians had to hear us – whether they wanted to or not. And you know what? It worked! Ofcom did change its policy and agreed to monitor diversity not just on-screen but also behind the camera.

The next problem was: how do you define 'diversity'? Just like the M5 to Devon on a Bank Holiday Monday, this was not going to be an easy journey.

8

HUMPTY DUMPTY SAT ON A WALL . . .

So far there is one group of people I have not mentioned in this book, and that is the small army of officials who work in the 'diversity and inclusion' departments across the media industry.

You've heard of 'em; they're usually people of colour, depressed, trapped in their office – alone, with a full waste-paper bin. Also lots of pictures that say things like 'Damn right, I *am* somebody!' This is usually situated next to one of a Black toddler weeping floods of tears over a pile of their hopes and dreams (inhales deeply, then continues).

Every UK broadcaster has a head of diversity or a diversity department tasked with trying to increase the 'diversity' in the company, usually part of a broader Human Resources department. Back in 2013, Barnie Choudhury, an Asian former BBC journalist formally asked, through a freedom of information request, how many schemes and efforts the BBC had rolled out in trying to increase racial diversity within the corporation, schemes often overseen by diversity departments. What he discovered was that in the fifteen years that preceded his freedom of information request, the BBC had launched at least (drumroll, fanfare – hundreds of non-White staff pulling their hair out) twenty-nine schemes! For those of you as mathematically challenged as I am, that is roughly one every six months, or, put another way, a new scheme every twenty-six weeks and six days.

During his time at the BBC, Barnie had actually taken part in not one but two of these schemes himself. He was clearly frustrated and disillusioned with all the different schemes that he felt had limited effect and did not help people like him. I suspect he was asking the question less out of academic curiosity and more to prove a point.

The BBC is far from alone in their diversity schemes delivering less than amazing results in the past.

It is a phenomenon we see repeated across industries and the world. Award-winning journalist Pamela Newkirk published an entire book in 2019 looking at the industry that has been built up around diversity. She called her book *Diversity, Inc.*, and the book's subtitle, *The Failed Promise of a Billion-Dollar Industry*, really says it all. It is replete with stories of how

– while the industry of diversity has grown – the actual numbers in the corporate world and in major public institutions have hardly shifted.

With the apparent lack of progress, it is very easy to be cynical about these people working in diversity and all the diversity departments. The fact of the matter is that all the folks I talk to working in this area are often more frustrated with the whole industry than anyone else. They typically do know 'where the bodies are buried' (metaphorically speaking, of course) and what works and what doesn't work.

Let me introduce you to Vimla (not her real name).

Vimla had a career in television production. After feeling that she had hit a glass ceiling, she left the department that made programmes, stayed within the same company and joined the department responsible for increasing the number of people from under-represented groups working for the organisation. That's right – she became one of 'those'. A diversity officer.

The irony of an Asian woman leaving a job making programmes behind the camera, where we are trying to increase diversity (*please don't tell me you skipped Chapter 7!*), to work in a department that is desperately trying to get people exactly like her into the very job she just left, was not lost on me or Vimla. But hey . . . just like President Trump claiming that George Floyd's ghost was looking down from heaven and silently applauding his actions in the midst of the riots, this actually happened.

Now, Vimla wasn't there when I gave my speech in Parliament urging Ofcom to monitor diversity behind the camera, but she heard about it and watched from afar as the regulator changed direction. She immediately felt apprehensive.

Despite working on it day in and day out, there is one word Vimla hates: 'diversity'.

'The problem with 'diversity' is that it means literally anything anybody wants it to mean.' She explained to me later. She referred to it as the *Alice in Wonderland* problem. In a famous passage in the children's story, Alice meets Humpty Dumpty. Their exchange goes like this:

'When *I* use a word,' Humpty Dumpty said, in rather a scornful tone, 'it means just what I choose it to mean – neither more nor less.'

'The question is,' said Alice, 'whether you *can* make words mean so many different things.'

'The question is,' said Humpty Dumpty, 'which is to be master – that's all.'

While we had got diversity written into the Charter, and even got Ofcom to agree to monitor diversity behind the camera – two massive wins – we had missed something.

We hadn't thought about defining diversity.

Vimla knew that in many ways we were living in a Wonderland, and she knew, like Humpty Dumpty did, that 'diversity' can mean almost anything that people want it to mean. Having a clear definition everyone agrees upon is essential.

Take the task of, for instance, trying to increase how many programmes are made outside of London. Ofcom can't actually monitor that number without a definition of what an 'out of London' production is. Ofcom first came up with a definition for this following the 2003 Communications Act which, amongst other things, sought to protect TV productions outside of London. As a result of this act, the major UK broadcasters (still) have to produce a certain percentage of their programmes outside of London. It's set out in their licence agreements.

Now, you would think creating a definition as to

whether a programme is made outside of London is pretty straightforward, but it's surprisingly complicated. So complicated, in fact, that Ofcom had to launch a public consultation on the question last year. Ofcom was concerned that its definition, which was almost ten years old by then, was being 'gamed' by production companies. For example, there had been allegations of some London-based production companies opening satellite offices outside of London to claim they were 'regional' just for one programme and then closing down immediately after the programme is completed. Similarly, there had been rumours of key production talent being shipped out of London to a hotel just for a few months in order to fit the definition.

It was not only production companies who were being accused of gaming the system. Ofcom was also concerned that some broadcasters might be intentionally turning a blind eye to productions they knew were not really 'regional' so they could have more freedom to commission and use whoever they want.

Although many people think the current definition has its flaws – which is why Ofcom held the consultation last year – having a clear definition has been essential in measuring how well broadcasters are doing in meeting their licence agreements, and holding them to account. When there isn't an agreed definition, or, in this case, if it's out of date, broadcasters can simply make up a definition that suits them and claim to be making progress, when in reality that's not the case at all.

This was the fear Vimla had when she heard that diversity was being written into the BBC Charter. She welcomed the idea, of course, but she was worried that we would simply end up in a Humpty Dumpty situation. Or to use another one of Vimla's favourite phrases, broadcasters would simply be 'marking their own homework'. Without a definition, how could Ofcom tell whether they had done well or not? Unless we provided one, how could we, the diversity mafia or even the general public, know if the broadcasters were really increasing diversity or just creating a definition that suited them in order to claim success?

There are some definitions of diversity that are already being used in the UK media industry. For instance, to qualify as a 'diverse' production for Channel 4, productions need to fulfil two different criteria from a complicated list. It's called a – wait for it – two-tick system.

The British Film Institute has a three-tick system, similar to Channel 4's, to decide whether a production is diverse or not. But the criteria the BFI says that a production has to choose from are quite different from the Channel 4 criteria.

BBC is even vaguer with its definition of 'diversity'. I know the BBC has a definition because, if you think back to the last chapter – do not tell me you skipped a chapter – the BBC told a Parliamentary Select Committee in 2015 that they were ring fencing money to develop diverse productions. So they must have known what a 'diverse production' was. But there did not seem to be a clear definition publicly available. On the BBC's own website it says the development fund will 'nurture talent (including presenters, actors, contributors and writers) and programme ideas that address areas of on-screen under-representation', though it does add 'for the first two years (2014–16) the fund will have a BAME focus'. Like Dominic Cumming's favourite hiking hat (very handy for castle visits), it is *all* a bit woolly.

My point here is that there is no industry-standard definition. And, as far as I am aware, none of the broad--casters have conducted open public consultations on how to define diversity. In short, the whole thing is a bit of a mess. They are all defining 'diversity' themselves and then – surprise, surprise – most of them are doing really well according to their own definition. 'We're doing great! Hoorah!'

Working day in and day out in diversity, Vimla saw the problem before I did. It soon became apparent that we needed to do something. I couldn't repeat the same trick again of going to the Houses of Parliament and leading everyone in a medley of Milli Vanilli hits, so I thought I would go to the politicians who might understand the importance of definitions more than most. The ones who are affected the most – albeit very differently – by the definitions of regional diversity: the Mayor of London and the First Minister of Scotland.

First stop was City Hall, where I sat down with Sadiq Khan and explained the problem to him. He was very sensitive to the issue for two reasons. First, in many ways London has lost out in the move to increase regional diversity. And second, London is one of the most diverse cities in Europe, with over 40 per cent of its population coming from a non-White background and having the largest Black population in the UK. Making sure that diversity works is a priority if you are overseeing a city like London.

The Mayor listened to our concerns and seemed to genuinely care about the issue and, as always, I went armed with a solution as to how we should define diversity. I had well and truly learned by this point to always have a possible solution up your sleeve. At the end of the meeting, the Mayor agreed to write an open letter to Ofcom saying they should define diversity.

A few days later, his letter was published in the *Guardian* newspaper with a possible definition that Ofcom could use and urging the regulator to set 'clear targets' or else 'progress cannot be properly assessed and tracked'. Job done.

I then jumped on a plane to Edinburgh to chat to Scotland's First Minister, Nicola Sturgeon. We sat down and discussed everything over a gallon mug of coffee and a few Tunnock's Teacakes. She completely grasped the problem of definitions straight away, and was eager to discuss the options for solutions. She has been involved with the politics of defining regional diversity for years.

The solution being easily agreed, that meant the second half of the meeting was taken up with a heated discussion around the best biscuits to serve at business meetings. I allowed her to win by agreeing that

Tunnock's Teacakes should be the victor as I wanted her to be on side but, dear readers, I secretly think very little beats a Rich Tea biscuit – they rock my world on a regular basis.

The end result couldn't have been better, with Nicola 'Tunnocks are the best' Sturgeon also agreeing to write a letter to Ofcom. Her letter was in many ways even stronger than the Mayor's letter, saying any diversity 'targets are unlikely to be met in the absence of robust definitions'.

I would love to finish this chapter by proclaiming another win and that Ofcom saw the error of its ways and rolled out a definition of diversity that is now used across the industry. But we are not at that stage yet.

Vimla is philosophical about it, as she's looked into the history. As I mentioned earlier, Ofcom came up with a definition of what constitutes an 'out of London' production in 2003. People living outside of London had been campaigning for this since at least the early 1990s. So Vimla tells me not to worry, this is just a first step.

She's right. Time is on our side. The whole experience taught me is that it is important to be *precise* about exactly what we are fighting for, and exactly how we measure success. It is also why I usually try not to use the word 'diversity' too much; instead I speak about specific groups.

The end goal might be an increase in diversity, but we get there by targeting specific under-represented groups. And no, I'm not talking about Boyz II Men, Fun Lovin' Criminals and New Edition. I'm talking about marginalised groups who have no skin in the game as yet.

Targeting them was *precisely* what I planned to do next.

8.5

THE UNBEARABLE DIVERSITY BURDEN OF LONELINESS

Before I get onto Chapter 9, I wanted to take a slight detour and talk about one of the most difficult issues facing people from marginalised and under-represented communities. And no, it isn't that thing where, if you're a Black person and you're some place where they don't actually know you, and a random person says, 'Hey, where you from?' and you say, 'Dudley,' and they go, 'No – where you *from*, from?' and you start explaining about being in your mum's tummy for nine or so months and they go, 'Bruv, where your *ancestors* from?'

It's not that.

I have tried to figure out where in the overall narrative of my political journey this chapter should fit . . . and that's because it kind of hangs over my entire career in television. It is at the start, middle, and if things don't change it will also be at the end. So I am a little stuck.

Yeah, so, the reason for the stuckness, the stuckiosity,

the stuckicity (if you will) is because it is a very personal confession, but a confession that I know a lot of people from 'diverse' backgrounds working in television can relate to.

A lot of the time, at work, I am lonely. Very lonely.
There. I said it. Phew.

Now, this is difficult to admit for two reasons. First, it feels like a major admission of failure. Just to give a little context – for what seemed like centuries, I was the only Black person on TV with his own show. I tell a lie – it was me and Trevor McDonald. I have regularly been the only Black person in meetings for over thirty years. I was the only Black person in the Cannon and Ball Summer Seasons. And I was the only *real* Black person in the *Black and White Minstrel Show*, summer and winter, circa 1975 to 1979. (For an insight into the suffering I endured, please purchase several copies of *Who Am I, Again?* and pass them around your friends. Misery loves company.)

It is lonely.

The second reason that being lonely is a hard admission to make is that I have also been worried about, and fear, the possibility that any of the brilliant people with whom I have worked in the showbiz trenches in sketches and sitcoms and random dramas, etc., might take my recently confessed loneliness (it was about a paragraph ago, remember?) as an insult. The truth is, I have rarely worked on a production, or been part of a team, where there hasn't been at least one friendly face or someone I would consider a friend. It's this apparent contradiction that goes to the heart of one of the unspoken issues regarding diversity – having large parts of your identity that you cannot share with your colleagues can distance you at work and ultimately create loneliness.

Although we're focusing on the media industry, the issues we're covering go far deeper and wider than just one sector and just one type of 'diversity'. As we were cooking up this book, and I was discussing this chapter with Marcus, he told me about his friend Will Norman. Will is a blind footballer who represented Great Britain at two Olympic Games (Beijing and London) and was part of the England team that won silver medals at the 2009 European Championships and the 2015 World Games in Seoul.

In many ways our lives (Will's and Lenny's) are a million miles apart – I do not know what it is like to be a gifted athlete or blind and Will doesn't know what it's like to a be 6 foot 3 inch Black man. But if

Will and I were to discuss loneliness, I'm pretty sure our worlds would collide!

Now, we've chosen to highlight Will because we didn't want the discussion around loneliness and diversity to be dismissed as just something that sad and unsuccessful people suffer from. Will is the definition of success. He's success-o-licious. Despite his sporting success, I am sure very few people will be surprised that blind football does not exactly pay the bills, and so for most of his life Will has worked in schools outreach trying to encourage young people from marginalised and under-represented groups to consider higher education as a realistic option. A job he finds very rewarding, despite how challenging it is.

Like me, he has often been the 'only one' at work. He has never worked professionally in an environment with other blind people. When we asked Will whether he feels lonely, his answer blew us away – Will's response to just our opening question was this:

Do I ever feel lonely? All the live-long day! But it's not what many people imagine loneliness to be. It's more like a feeling of homelessness, of unbelonging, a sense that this is not my land, that I'm a traveller, passing through, for ever restless. You can stop for a while, you can enjoy generous hospitality, but you are always a guest, often welcome, but never at home.

There is a loneliness that comes from being openly discriminated against, shut out, but there's a subtler, creeping loneliness that comes from operating in environments that think they've got your back, that want to be inclusive and participatory, but that don't see the thousand tiny ways in which the way they operate causes you problems every single day. This creeping version – the loneliness of a thousand cuts – stems, I guess, from the feeling that whatever you do, the world was set up by someone else to suit *their* needs, not yours. It's not your world. You can live in it, but only if you are prepared to accept their terms and conditions.

I don't want to give even vaguely the merest smidge of an impression that I have any idea what it might be like to be blind because I am Black or vice versa. That is the whole point. We feel lonely precisely because *other people cannot know what our lives are like*. It's the whole 'walking a mile in someone else's shoes' deal. If you haven't done it, you'll never understand what it feels like.

Reading Will's testimony was an incredibly cathartic experience; I began to fully understand that the loneliness I felt in the work environment was not just a 'Black thing', but a 'diversity thing'. Not only that, Will identified something I have struggled to articulate for years. It's the idea of our diversity being championed but ultimately feeling hollow inside. He talks about it in terms of disability; I often feel it as a Black man. To quote Will again:

> When you first start working somewhere, the fact that you bring a different perspective is welcomed, even celebrated, and there's an eagerness to get to know you, what your disability means to you, and how it might be able to help shape the organisation for the better. That's a really great attitude and I applaud it entirely, but there's a danger that an organisation can tire of it once they feel they've learned everything they want to learn, and come to understand everything they can be bothered to understand about you. It's vampiric: once you've been drained of all useful knowledge, you can feel as if you have been set aside. Of course, for a blind person, being blind isn't novel, it isn't interesting, and it isn't a 'useful perspective to feed into a

strategic document', it's a state of existence, today, tomorrow, and every other day. We don't get to cast it aside once we're bored.

Even during the good times, when you are very much celebrated for what you bring to the table as a blind person, there's a sense that actually it's not about you, it's about what other people can use you for. It's like that cliché about the hollowness of celebrity. We want you to attend this event as a VIP, but can you come as a Paralympian, not as Will Norman?

Now I know what some people might be think-ing at this point: 'Oi! Henry! *No!* Not everything's about diversity, dude. Any and everybody can suffer from loneliness.' That is true, but although anyone can suffer from loneliness at work, what I'm trying to express is that loneliness through our careers is a disproportionate and constant experience of people from under-represented backgrounds.

People from diverse backgrounds – such as ethnic minority groups and disabled people – are more at risk of suffering from loneliness, which can perpetu-ate or aggravate mental health issues and many other problems faced by these people already.

The follow-up question you probably have now, though, is, 'Why does it matter?' Who cares? Does it affect other people? Does loneliness actually affect anyone's career? I mean, are Will and I just being ungrateful for the career opportunities we've received?

Well, Gallup regularly conducts employee engagement work surveys, and one of the key questions they ask is: 'Do you have a best friend at work?' They ask it for a very good reason. Steve Miranda of Cornell University's Center for Advanced HR Studies (a pre-eminent institution focused on work, employment and labour), when commenting on people without 'best friends at work' said in an interview in 2014 'people who are lonely and disengaged at work deliver far less discretionary effort than people who have a support system or a go-to person [at work].' Loneliness not only affects the career prospects of the worker but, in turn, also affects the performance of the company the lonely person is working for. A 2018 American study also concluded that 'co-workers can recognise this loneliness and see it hindering team member effectiveness'. However, they rarely understand the reasons behind this loneliness and instead just want to get rid of the 'underperforming' colleague.

It can become a vicious cycle as people from under-represented backgrounds are more likely to be lonely, which means they underperform and are less likely to be promoted and more likely to be let go . . . leading to more loneliness for the next person who comes along and hopes it will be different.

So, can we ever solve this problem?

Well, you won't be surprised to know that there is another reason Will was chosen as our featured 'lonely guy' in this chapter. Because as well as being able to talk about what it is like to be lonely in the corporate world, he is able to offer a unique insight on what it is like for a disabled person to be part of a majority on a successful team . . . because when he puts on a football jersey, all his teammates are also blind.

As if to underline the findings of the academic studies that say people do not perform at their best when they are lonely, Will told us quite honestly:

> The only times in my life I have felt centred,
> harmonised, and in a state of flow have been
> those times when I have been in a visually
> impaired environment with other blind people;
> the rest of the time it's like I'm living life in
> translation, which obviously takes a lot of

extra work. It's hard to do justice to the size of the void between the two feelings. Really it comes down to the difference between feeling at home in your own skin, and feeling like a visitor – a stranger in a strange land.

It is this unique perspective that many Paralympians in team sports possess – knowing how they perform when they are in a majority environment versus when they are in a minority – that we wanted Will to explain further.

And what we realised is that much of the negative feeling about loneliness is also about powerlessness.

Although in my day-to-day work I am the only blind person in the room, in the football squad our blindness was not only something we shared, it was the sport's very reason for being. This was a very empowering feeling, and went beyond the players themselves. The staff too, themselves all fully sighted, owed their positions to the fact that we were blind. I remember once, in a heated exchange with one of the coaches, saying, 'My blindness is the only reason you're here wearing the three lions. Without me and my disability, you're just another footballing wannabe with a whistle.'

I, Lenny Henry, have never been much of an athlete – although in my neighbourhood, my downward-facing dog is the envy of all Great Danes within a forty-mile radius. The idea of needing other Black people around me so I can feel empowered and combat the feelings of loneliness is something I have been working towards. I've set up two different production companies – and part of the reason I did that was so that I might possibly be able to work with other Black people. To not to be the only one in the room.

Long before I started on this political journey to increase diversity, I organised a three-day writer's initiative called 'A Step Forward'. This was back in the early 1990s. It was funded by the BBC and aimed at BAME and working-class writers. The great and the good came and spoke to the new talent and the whole thing generated a new group of writers, some of whom would wind up writing on *The Real McCoy*, a Black sketch show that played at prime time on BBC2 and ran for six years.

Through that group, my production company Crucial Films was able to hire diverse crew and production staff; we made *Funky Black Shorts* and *Crucial Tales* and *Neverwhere*. I met my first cinematographer of colour, Remi Adefarasin (a lovely bloke and a proper talent), when he shot the first season of *Chef!*

Now, all good things come to an end and Crucial Films did so in 1998. I'm not writing about this to bemoan the fact that Crucial Films is no more or to reminisce about the good old days. What that experience gave me was, just like Will Norman's football career, a sense of just how positive it can be to be surrounded by people that resemble you.

Will also looks back at his football experience and like me is quite sanguine about the whole affair, saying:

> Ultimately, though, you can't live for ever in a bubble, lest it become a ghetto. There's a balance to be struck. It's important to have time within your own community so that you can develop friendships and support networks that will see you through the tough times, as well as learning where your strengths really lie when measured against your true peers. But you can't stay there for ever, because without integration we'll never develop the mutual

understanding and immunity to ignorance
that we need if we're ever going to be able to
call ourselves a truly diverse society.

For me, combating this type of loneliness is really about balance and a question of choice. The fight to increase diversity and representation in all walks of life is one where under-represented people should be able to sometimes choose environments where they feel empowered and are unquestionably in the majority. If we choose to step out of those environments, the only option available should not be one where we have to be in a minority of one. My fight for diversity is to make both choices possible and even desirable. To give people real choices. To avoid loneliness.

Which is precisely why I finally decided to take my diversity campaign to the very top – and no, I'm not talking about the guest bathroom at Gary Barlow's house.

I'm talking about *10 Downing Street*.

9

SO NEAR AND YET SO FAR

Let me introduce you to Nadine Marsh-Edwards.

If Carlton Dixon (in Chapter 3) is a rarity in the UK film industry – Black, comprehensive school educated, working class – Nadine is all these things but an even larger outlier. Wait for it . . . a *woman*! (Cue fanfare, firework display, Cirque du Soleil acrobats, toddlers on bungee ropes, Beyoncé singing 'Run the World' . . .)

And she is not just *any* woman. She is one of the most successful independent UK film producers. She has been producing and executive producing award-winning films since the 1980s. She breaks barriers the way Lewis Hamilton breaks speed limits – effortlessly. Her films *Looking for Langston* and *Young Soul Rebels* had Black gay characters and explored gay themes in the 1980s and early 1990s at the same time that the Conservative government was bringing in Clause 28 to restrict the teaching of gay issues in schools. We're talking tough here!

Tougher and more solid than Sly Stallone's lower abs in *Rocky II*.

Her film *Bhaji on the Beach* had young Asian women and Black men falling in love and in central roles back in 1993 – the same year that bigoted thugs killed Stephen Lawrence, a horrific murder that exposed systemic racism in the Metropolitan Police force and other British public institutions. She was way ahead of her time, and still is today. Her 2018 film on Netflix, *Been So Long*, starring Michaela Coel, is just brilliant. Crucially, as well as being one of the country's top independent film producers, Nadine is also passionate about increasing diversity in the film industry both in front of the camera and behind it. For her, it is personal.

It is almost impossible to state the array of challenges facing Black women in the industry behind the camera – but we're gonna give it the old college try anyway. Let's just look at the problems facing all women. Marcus? Come forward with the statistical lyrics!

According to the film data researcher Stephen Follows, in 2018 just over a quarter (26.4 per cent) of all producing credits on feature films went to women. Now if you think that number is bad, once you start to break down what we *mean* by 'all producing credits' things get even worse.

The bulk of that 26.4 per cent is made up of 'associate producer', 'co-producer', 'assistant producer' and 'line producer' credits. When you look at the all-important 'producer' and 'executive producer' credits, women don't even make up a fifth of those mentioned in dispatches.

OK, let's slice and dice the figures to make them even more depressing. The few women who *are* fortunate enough to produce films are less likely to produce high-budget films and are invariably pushed into genres with less money. During 1990–2018, the number of women producing action films, where invariably the big bucks are at (your *Mission Impossibles*, your *Bourne* franchises, your Christopher Nolan bangers), accounted for roughly 15 per cent of producers.

Now, so far we've been talking about women in general, so let's get a bit more specific so that this pertains to Nadine, this chapter's subject. Here are some stats for *Black* women producers.

SECTION TO BE FILLED IN

(Message from editor: 'Lenny, there's just an empty space – I've been waiting for weeks for you to fill in these stats – what's going on?'

Me: Smiley emoji with question mark over head.)

The reason we are publishing the book without the stats for Black women producers in the UK is that there are *so few of them* that the stats just don't exist – or at least Marcus and I can't find them. I've been working in the industry for half a century and can literally count the number of Black women producers on one hand. That is why Nadine is so amazing – she's a real superhero who has beaten the odds time and time again in so many different ways.

In 1990, if you were a woman and got any type of producer credit, the chances of you getting a second one in the next five years were less than 1.5 per cent. I have no idea what the probability was for a Black woman, but I am guessing they had a higher chance of marrying into the Royal family. So really Nadine is on the same footing as Meghan Markle. Or all three of the Three Degrees.

The important thing to remember is you can't survive as an independent film producer for over thirty years and consistently beat the odds time and time again unless you understand how the business side of the industry works and are able to turn a profit. That makes Nadine even rarer.

While waiting to see if Ofcom would create a

definition for diversity for the broadcasters to use, there was no way Marcus and I were going to sit on our laurels. As Nadine's example illustrates, there was just way too much to do. Fate works in mysterious ways. I received an invitation to give a speech at MIPCOM – a massive global television event held in Cannes, France, where the real business of television takes place with broadcasters and media companies around the world buying and selling programmes and different formats. This is that hallowed industry event where the business meets the show.

If I was going to accept the invitation, I needed to generate a speech and table an idea that would resonate and be relevant to these business people. Not just a Mark Ronson-style remix of my previous outings. And that, my friends, is how the idea of diversity tax breaks was born.

Here's the skinny. Right now, certain governments around the world give tax breaks to movie and television productions to encourage producers to film in their countries. It is why remote locations you've never heard of are sometimes popular film locations – did you know the game show *Total Wipeout* is filmed in Argentina? Or that most of *Game of Thrones* was filmed in Ireland? It wasn't because their producers just wanted a non-glamorous holiday. The tax breaks are meant to encourage productions to base themselves and film in a location they would not normally choose for the advantageous cut in taxes. Sounds good, right?

Even if the countries get less tax from each production company, they believe that just having the next big blockbuster movie, or high-end TV drama, choosing them for production bases or locations, etc., is good news for their local economies, because the film and television productions employ shedloads of people and there are a whole heap of other businesses that benefit from a movie or series being made – i.e. catering, hotels or even tourism, bars, clubs, pubs, etc.

Tax breaks in the film and television industry in the UK have been seen to work. Tax breaks began to be used in the film and creative industries back in 2007; since then, employment in the industry has grown by 5 per cent on average every year and now provides nearly 2 million jobs in the country. That compares to just 1.2 per cent overall employment growth in the rest of the UK. Yet, while tax breaks have been great for the industry as a whole, they haven't been great for diversity. Diversity numbers have hardly budged since they were introduced. Like Dominic Cummings in a traffic jam on a bank holiday, diversity numbers are stationary.

So that's what I decided to present to MIPCOM. I sat down once more with Marcus and, over a few coffees, bagels and those fantastic croissants with the almonds dotted over them like jewels, we crafted a speech proposing the principle of giving tax breaks to productions that meet certain diversity criteria when filming in UK territories. For example, if there were a Black screenwriter, a female director or a percentage of disabled people employed, then the production could qualify for an additional tax break. We tied the idea up with a bow and I delivered the speech at MIP-COM. There was polite applause. I think the *Financial Times* covered the idea and then . . .

. . . it effectively sank without trace.

I knew it was a good idea, though. I inherently like the idea of rewarding good practice. Like Super Nanny always says, 'reward the good behaviour and ignore the bad'. So the notion of tax breaks for diversity sat on the naughty step for a while; Marcus and I had some rethinking to do.

I wondered if something was wrong. We gathered a posse of smart people from all walks of life, a gathering of Black, Asian, some able-bodied, some with disabilities – all passionate about issues regarding across-the-board inclusion. When you assemble a room of diverse people in terms of optics *and* opinions – people from all walks of life with all sorts of different experiences – things work out better.

Nadine, one of the best businesswomen in the industry, was part of this conclave of smart folks, and I asked her for her honest feedback on our idea. She not only convinced me that we were on the right track, but also made me think how we could tweak the policy, giving different types of tax breaks or even credits to different types of productions. Don't worry, I won't lay out all the details here. Tax can be boring at the best of times, but it is enough to say that I was convinced we should keep on pushing the idea.

This time we would go straight to the top. If we wanted tax breaks, we had to go beyond making the case to a bunch of semi-powerful, Danish pastry-eating business mavens congregated in the South of France. We were going to take it to the Prime Minister (I can't even remember who it was at the time. I think it was Theresa May – y'know? Tried to teach Kenyan kids to boogie. Ye Gods . . .).

And for that we needed some real drama, something to get people to sit up and listen – make a real splash.

Marcus and I drafted a letter, and sent it around a few trusted business people – such as Nadine – who rewrote and perfected it. Then, we launched a three-pronged attack.

One: We organised a small group of us to hand-deliver the letter to 10 Downing Street. The group should include a few high-profile faces in the media industry, as well as a few highly respected industry figures whose work takes place behind the camera rather than in front. The final magnificent seven were Meera Syal (excellent actor and writer behind *Goodness Gracious Me*, *Bhaji on the Beach*, *Life Isn't All Ha Ha Hee Hee* – that's a real title, btw), Adrian Lester (Soul Brother number one, top dramatic actor), Ade Adepitan (one of the UK's most recognisable Black and disabled presenters), Angela Ferreira (former head of the BBC's Afro-Caribbean Unit and former Channel 4 commissioner, now MD of Douglas Road productions), Nadine Marsh-Edwards, Marcus Ryder and of course myself. (Pat Younge, former head of TV production at the BBC, was also meant to be there as he had helped with the letter but he was unavailable on the day.)

Two: We would do a media blitz on the day we delivered the letter, making sure we got to appear on as many news programmes as possible.

The following day a smaller group of us met with members of the opposition, specifically Dawn Butler MP, the Shadow Equalities Minister at the time, and John McDonnell, the Shadow Chancellor of the Exchequer. I asked for Hank Marvin and Bruce Welch from the actual Shadows to be in attendance, but was shouted down once more. Being in a pressure group is hard work.

We met with Ms Butler and co because the issue of diversity tax breaks (in our minds) has to be bigger than party politics. It is a solution that should be implemented irrespective of who is in government. The fact it was a smaller group was no indication of how important we all felt this second meeting was, but more to do with pre-existing diary commitments.

It was going great – then we stumbled.

While everyone loved the idea in principle, they (particularly Treasury guys) all had one question: What economic modelling have you done on this? Can you point to the academic work or economic analysis that shows that your strategy would be a success?

We pointed to the statistics I quoted earlier about the increase in people working in the film industry since the UK has adopted film and TV tax breaks in general. There is also a great study that was done for the National Endowment for Science, Technology and the Arts that looked at a tax scheme in Manchester rolled out in 2009 to encourage innovation in website design and advertising to see if the tax breaks really did what they set out to do or whether they just put a bit more money into company directors' pockets.

In this study they randomly gave tax credits to 150 eligible firms and compared them to another 301 equally eligible firms who they did not give tax credits to. This particular enterprise was a randomised controlled trial, a new technique for which Esther Duflo, Abijit Banerjee and Michael Kremer were awarded the Nobel Prize for Economics in 2019. They're the gold standard for testing if a tax policy – or any government policy, for that matter – actually works.

The study for the Manchester scheme found that tax credits worked when it came to the creative industry! The companies who got the tax credits increased their innovation by 16 per cent and they made more money overall.

I thought we had the evidence and academic studies to prove it would work. They came back with the same response: 'Can you prove it will work for *diversity*? How do we know we won't just be giving away

money and not getting any more diversity in return?'
When you are talking about tax breaks to Treasury
officials, while they may care about diversity issues,
their primary focus is on balancing the books. Tax
concerns win and lose elections, so politicians need to
know they are on to a winner with additional proof
that it will work.

We couldn't *prove* tax breaks would work when
it came to diversity. Every time the question was
raised, we stumbled. We indicated examples in the
US where they have tied their film tax breaks to
certain diversity criteria. We were able to point to
France, where film grants received a boost if they met
certain criteria. But they could see through us. The
simple answer was: none of the countries in question, including the UK, had conducted *any* rigorous
economic analysis on the impact of diversity tax
breaks on their film and TV industries. We had not
contacted any financial or tax experts to write any
papers on the subject. We came up empty-handed.
Indeed, while the majority of tax initiatives don't
actually have a great deal of decent academic work
behind them, we had to take this challenge seriously because we were proposing something brand new,
never before tested in the UK.

I thought about Nadine and how she must have had to convince hard-nosed business people time and again why her diverse and inclusive films could make money, not because they had any specific love for Black and Asian representation in movies. And I realised I had to do the same. It was a tough lesson for me. We had planned out everything so well but we hadn't done one part of our homework.

I vowed I would never let this happen again . . .

(Next stop: What if there was some kind of Diversity Research Centre in broadcast media based somewhere like – y'know – Birmingham – maybe affiliated to a university up there? A place that could prevent further embarrassments due to lack of supporting evidence for any subject to do with diversity tax breaks, ring-fenced money, etc. *ever happening again*? Hmmmmmmmmm . . . wow that's a 'long brackets section', innit, Marcus?)

10

DON'T MOURN – MOBILISE!

If there is one underlying theme to this book it is that every success relies on teamwork, actually putting the idea of diversity into practice. That two heads are better than one. And ten heads from a variety of backgrounds are better than two from the same background with similar experiences. Many a mickle makes a muckle; if you want to lift yourself up, lift up someone else. (Booker T. Washington said that. I preferred it when he led the MGs; we'll talk about that some other time).

So far, the teams that had brought our successes, rewritten important speeches, drafted new policy solutions, that had delivered the tax breaks letter to Downing Street, had all been assembled in an 'as and when' methodology – it had all been incredibly *ad hoc*.

I was frustrated that diversity tax breaks hadn't been adopted by the government and some of our bigger proposals such as ring-fenced funds had only been partially adopted. We had come a long way, but when I actually stopped to look around, I saw that someone had sneakily redirected us almost back to the beginning. Bah!

In the words of the anti-apartheid movement of the 1980s: 'Don't mourn. Mobilise!' I knew we couldn't just give up, but I also knew we couldn't continue by just relying on me calling up friends any more. We needed to mobilise!

As always, the solution came over a random conversation with Marcus with two things coming together at once. We were discussing parenthood and how nothing really prepares you for it. You end up relying on grandparents, aunts, uncles, family friends – basically, anyone who has gone through the process before and didn't drop their child on their head (or at least not too many times). (The 'not dropping the child on the head' test is one of the most important hoops all fam and friends must jump through before being allowed to babysit your child. Trust me, bruv.) To use business parlance: all these friends and family have what is called 'institutional memory'. They have seen it all before, they know what works and what doesn't. They are Yoda; you are Luke.

Whether you are trying to raise a child in a small family or roll out a new policy to increase the number of women or Black or Brown people working in a company, institutional memory makes all the difference. It can be the difference between a business repeating a costly mistake or knowing best practice that has worked in the past and being able to use it.

However, when it comes to diversity in the media industry it can feel like we have no institutional memory. I cannot remember a time in my forty-plus-year career when women, Black, Asian and disabled people have not been actively fighting for a bigger place at the media table to tell their stories and have their voices heard.

Yet, when I talk to senior industry figures in their fifties, sixties and even seventies, who have been at the front line trying to increase diversity in television, I am amazed how consistently they feel that the present policies rolled out by broadcasters are either repeating the same mistakes or failing to capitalise on what has happened before.

So let me introduce the last character in the book, one who comes from a demographic that is all too often overlooked when it comes to the whole diversity debate: the 6 per cent. That's right. Let me introduce you to a White, seventy-year-old, heterosexual man living in London: Simon Albury.

A flamboyant character with a shock of white hair – you can normally tell Simon is in the building due to his booming voice, brightly coloured spectacles and effortless swag. He heads an organisation called the Campaign for Broadcasting Equality and works tirelessly to increase diversity in broadcasting. The way he describes himself on Twitter sums him up the best: 'I can speak out because I am privileged, retired & have nothing to lose.' He's like the living embodiment of that film *The Expendables*.

It is what he did *before* he retired that I think is most valuable. He was firmly embedded in the television establishment. He was a producer for current affairs programmes, worked for both the BBC and ITV, and had been in TV for over thirty years. After his TV career, he took up the post of CEO of the Royal Television Society. Diversity and inclusion-wise, Simon's a 'big piece of equipment' as they'd say in the *Breaking Bad* writer's room.

As well as being a White heterosexual male at the very core of the industry, he has also been involved at pivotal moments when the industry has undergone seismic changes. He was key to independent television companies being given more power and fundamentally changing the relationship between broadcasters and the companies who actually make the programmes.

It is his thirty-plus years' experience that makes him so important when there are discussions around the demarginalisation of media diversity. When he talks about representation in our industry, he is not some old curmudgeon who thinks 'everything was better in my day'. Invariably, people like Simon can offer a relevant critique on what broadcasters are doing right and what they are doing wrong. I cannot tell you how often a conversation about a new diversity policy with Simon will start like this: 'The new policy initiative is OK, though it is similar to what we tried in 1995, and where it went wrong was XX, so if I were in their shoes I would try YY.' Or he will say, 'I don't know why the broadcasters are dismissing that policy approach; it worked perfectly well in the eighties and, with a bit of tweaking, I think we might have something.'

We need to harness the experience of those who have been at the heart of the industry and that includes not only the people from under-represented backgrounds, but also pioneers like Simon. Far too few people with this institutional memory and experience are being consulted about the various diversity policies that the different broadcasters roll out every year. We lose this institutional memory at our peril, and with increased freelancing, staff turnover and the end of jobs for life, the situation is only going to get worse.

And so we came up with an idea (well, Marcus did – I stood back in awe and then rushed to pay homage to his bad-ass self). Could we create a diversity 'brains trust' that would capture all the institutional memory and make sure we build on all the best practice that has gone before it and avoid all the mistakes? And while we were discussing that, the solution to our diversity tax breaks became obvious. What if this brains trust was housed in one of the UK's top media universities? That would mean that as well as being a brains trust of media diversity practice – good and bad – over the years, it would also have the academic and intellectual credibility to analyse new policies. Crunch the numbers. Even do economic modelling. (I think you can see where we're going with this.) It would be comprised of about eight to ten key people who had either worked in the UK film and television industry for the last four to five decades or were serious academic heavyweights. Or both!

Marcus put out a call to academics and media professionals to see if anyone would be interested in such an institution. The response was great, and about a dozen of them met in a bar a stone's throw from the BBC's New Broadcasting House in London (the location seemed appropriate enough) to discuss the idea. No one did Jägerbombs or a back somersault off the bar and into a nearby bin, but a good time was had by all.

There was just one thing missing – we didn't have a university.

Luckily enough for us, one of the professors present was Professor Diane Kemp. She had been involved in work on media diversity in academia for over ten years. Before that, she had been a journalist, and constantly on the frontline in the fight to increase diversity. After this, quite frankly, gorgeous meeting of like-minded academics and media professionals everything went quiet for a few months. Then suddenly, out of the blue, Professor Kemp called Marcus and me with some good news. She had somehow convinced the Vice Chancellor of her institution – Birmingham City University – to house the institution and now was trying to get them to stump up some cash.

The whole thing was perfect – just like pieces of a puzzle falling into place. Birmingham City University is one of the leading media universities in the country. And Birmingham is one of the most racially diverse cities in the country – and is not London. As a location for a diversity brains trust it felt like the perfect location. At this point, I should declare a slight interest in Birmingham City University. Not only am I from Dudley – which is just outside Birmingham – but I have been the Chancellor of the university since 2016. I know! Cool, right? I get to wear the robes and everything and make speeches – it's like if Dumbledore was from the Black Country and had Jamaican parents. Get in!

It is precisely because I am Chancellor that I did not go to the university to talk to the Vice Chancellor about our plans. I didn't want to use that position in any way. So it was a complete shock when Prof Kemp told us she had spoken to her bosses. She told us that it wasn't quite a done deal. The Vice Chancellor wanted to meet Marcus and me to talk through what we envisaged for the institution. He was the guy holding the purse strings and, therefore, he was the one who could say yea or nay.

The four of us met – we had snacks and tiny espressos – and the rest, as they say, is history. He agreed to set up the Centre for Media Diversity and initially fund it for at least the first five years. The one condition he set was he wanted my name on the door. He thought after all the campaigning I had been involved in on the issue, my name might be able to attract more funding and publicity. And so it became the 'Sir Lenny Henry Centre for Media Diversity'. We shook on it. Marcus bagged all the leftover snacks for his next meeting with Simon Albury – and everyone was happy.

It was November 2019, we would announce the Centre in 2020 and launch in March. We sent out invites – we were inundated! Everybody from the media industry wanted to come. We were oversubscribed within hours. We had some extremely high-powered executives asking me if I could source them tickets – I felt like Beyoncé handing out afterparty passes. This was going to be the biggest launch since Apollo 11. What could possibly go wrong?

Just a random question: anyone heard of Covid-19? Tiny little virus that turned the world upside down? Everybody two metres apart, forbidden to travel, no sneezing, coughing, droplets or touching. Lot of handwashing. Remember that?

Ahhh . . . right . . .

OK, well, the pandemic affected everything. Our physical launch had to be migrated online and we had to send out launch videos to everyone instead. We did save a whole heap of cash on the buffet though, so that's a bonus.

And that's when the really unglamorous work began. No high-profile letters to 10 Downing Street. No leading everyone in a medley of Milli Vanilli hits. And definitely no excruciating puns.

After we launched, the management board met almost every week for the first two months to work out what we should focus on and work out our best course of action. We decided from the start that we didn't want the Centre to be a campaigning or advocacy organisation. We wanted it to conduct rigorous academic research that could analyse what worked and what didn't in terms of increasing all forms of diversity in the industry. To literally just be a 'brains trust'.

To this end there would be four work streams. We would have a qualitative work stream – interviewing people about their personal experiences in the industry. This was about systematically capturing the institutional memory that is all too often lost when it comes to diversity. We would have a quantitative work stream – people crunching the numbers and doing the hard statistical analysis. If we ever campaign for diversity tax breaks again, it will be because the

Centre has done the economic modelling and proved it works. As I am writing today, the Centre hasn't yet done the modelling – and as passionate as I am about diversity tax breaks, I didn't push the rest of the board to put it in our first tranche of work. The centre needs to be independent of any agenda I might have and there are many other pressing issues to look at.

The third work stream was organising industry events so we could all talk to one another and share best practice. And the last work stream only came up when Dr David Dunkley Gyimah, a senior lecturer at Cardiff University, suggested launching a journal together so we could publish works by both seasoned and young academics and media professionals on how to increase the number of under-represented groups in the industry.

The Centre is in its infancy and I am still nervous writing about it. There is so much that can go wrong. But if there is one thing I have learnt in this crazy journey it is not to be scared. The only way you avoid failure is by not trying. We might make mistakes, but we refuse not to try to make the media industry more diverse and more representative of under-represented groups. And, in our small way, make the UK in general a fairer and more equitable place to live.

Every victory we have experienced in the last seven years has been coupled with a mistake and every failure has provided a lesson upon which we can build. With the Centre – our new 'brains trust' – we are simply at the next stage of the journey. The Centre and my campaigning work are separate, but the Centre will subject any of our policy solutions, as well as policies suggested by broadcasters, to independent analysis.

Never again would we be in the position where someone could dismiss any idea we'd had because it lacked economic modelling or academic credibility.

When I enter a room representing my colleagues of all hues, genders and abilities in the industry, I intend to be metaphorically standing on the shoulders of giants who have preceded me – calling on the institutional memory of years of collective experience. Experience of Black and Asian people who have worked in the industry, disabled people, women, LGBTQ+ people and, yes, White heterosexual men from London like Simon Albury. Add to that, the work of the best economists and business academics – with such intelligence backing us up, I should be able to step up to any podium, whether at BAFTA, Cannes, the Royal Television Society, or even 10

Downing Street, and be able to talk confidently, with evidence-based testimony, and no one will be able to ignore what we are saying.

This, indeed, feels like a possible road to many defeats before we have a victory. As Maya Angelou wrote, 'You may encounter many defeats, but you must not be defeated.' We'll keep going, whatever the weather, whatever shade gets thrown, no matter how hard the road because this idea of a level playing field is worth it. So let's get levelling.

11

POWER TO THE PEOPLE

And . . . exhale!

In many ways, working on this book has been a kind of therapy. It serves as a document charting the arduous journey from my silly 'it'll be all White on the night' joke at the BAFTAs way back in 2013 to a full (ish) political awakening.

I have to tell you, it has been a real awakening. I'm a completely different person than I was when I came out with that awful pun. I've become simultaneously a little bit more hopeful, a little bit more cynical and a whole heap more wise.

This book was not purely an exercise in personal catharsis – there would have been easier ways to tackle my demons and give me a little bit more insight about what on earth has happened in my life over the last eight years. (The weight loss, the weight gain, even more weight loss, much more weight gain – rinse and repeat – I was like Oprah Winfrey watching her life flash before her eyes). Also, just for the record, as someone who has been on TV since I was a teenager, I would strongly recommend that people do not undergo therapy in public. (Buses going by, passers-by commenting on the analysis, 'That'll be because your mum beat you with a shoe when you were four,' stray dogs howling just as you reach a breakthrough . . .) Leave it to professionals and the privacy of a psychiatrist's couch.

No. The real reason we decided to write this book was to provide a blueprint or a road map for how to campaign. Specifically, how to campaign to increase representation of all marginalised people in the media industry and, more broadly, across the country's boardrooms and everywhere the positions of power are held by the usual dominant-culture faces. Which really brings to me the culmination of the whole book. (No, missus, this *isn't* the bit where Len does a triple back flip off the bar at Nando's and lands in Marcus's back pocket.) Dear reader, this book is fundamentally about (cue drumroll) power.

Work on this book began just before Christmas 2019; however, on 25 May 2020, the world was turned upside down when George Floyd, a Black man, was killed by a White American police officer kneeling on his neck for eight minutes and forty-six seconds. This was also during a time when the entire world had been turned upside down by a pandemic – Covid-19 – that continues to rage across societies.

We have all seen the George Floyd video footage and it *has* changed the world. I hope permanently for the better. When I watched it, I saw someone just a few years younger than me, a man who resembled me, who could have been me, who was utterly powerless. We watched someone's life being stolen from them. I thought of the bystanders, hovering around the wrongdoing policemen, utterly powerless to stop the killing they could see occurring right in front of their eyes. The best they could do was to plead helplessly and bear witness by filming the event.

I won't write what I think about the killing in any detail on this particular outing. People far more eloquent, and with greater insight, have already written copious amounts about the George Floyd murder. The subject deserves its own book.

But, between you and me, the killing made me come to realise that, in many ways, I have been using the wrong words to describe what we have been trying to achieve over the last few years. I did tell you about my habitual manner of learning from my repeated mistakes, didn't I? Did you *really* think you'd escape without some kind of 'Len's One to Grow On' moment? Hah!

What we are trying to achieve is not just better 'representation'. Or a few more Black and Brown faces, or other minorities in a few key jobs. What the death of George Floyd made me realise is what we are trying to achieve is power.

In that terrible video, we saw people with power – the police – acting with perceived impunity against people with no power at all. In the campaign work and lobbying we've all been doing in the last few years, the purpose and intention has always been to shift power, significantly, from those who have almost all of it, to those who have almost none.

Controversially, I don't believe the mass protests seen around the world over George Floyd and Black Lives Matter are happening simply because suddenly everybody has had a Road to Damascus (my least favourite Hope, Crosby and Lamour movie) moment about anti-racism. There is no doubt it has provided the impetus for a powerful anti-racism movement, but I also believe that it moved all those people deep down because there are far too many of us who are powerless – and people could see how important it is for Black people to have more power.

That impotence that too many of us feel – to a greater or lesser degree – might manifest itself in various different forms: a lack of diversity in the TV industry, or huge pay gaps for women even when they are represented on top company boards, or even Black people suffering disproportionately from Covid-19 in societies where they are minorities.

The real problem is about power: who has it, and who doesn't.

Since BAFTA pun-gate in 2013, my diversity crime-fighting partner, Marcus, and I have been trying to find ways to level this uneven power playing field. To find a method of protest that encourages a shift from the dominant culture whereby they – the 6 per cent – begin to share power more broadly. And when they don't want to share it (when do they ever?) we find ways for all of us to take it.

When it comes to broadcast media (film, TV, radio, journalism, etc.), we're trying to figure out a way for an entire industry to be restructured so that Black and Brown people, and all the other minorities – the 96 per cent – can feel empowered. This is not just about one or two more jobs. This is not just about one more Black commissioner. This is about power. We need to methodically restructure the entire television and media industry so that there is a more equal sharing of power. Relax! It's not a power grab. people, it's a power *share* ...

Remember the BAFTA award acceptance speech made by Joaquin Phoenix at the very start of the book? He spoke about 'systemic racism' in the film industry. What we need is fundamental, integral, *systemic* change. Can I get a 'Hallelujah'?

Hallelujah!

I've learnt the hard way that this kind of seismic shift does not come overnight. That's what we're not only arguing for but also developing strategies for. Real, concrete, actionable ideas. In my own industry, media, this means we are not simply asking for executives to be 'less racist, less sexist or less ableist' in the programmes they may or may not produce. We're not even asking them simply to be anti-racist or anti-sexist or anti-ableist (although that wouldn't hurt).

We're asking them to go the extra mile. To enable every under-represented group to have the power and resources to produce, write and make the kind of programmes we perceive to be commission-worthy. We want to make programmes, tell stories, using our own unique perspective. We want to set the frameworks for the analysis of the news, not just to present the news or repeatedly be its tragic subject matter.

Every industry and organisation will have its own analogous specific applications. We need to begin systematically identifying what permanent change means across *all* sectors and then find the tools to enable the shift in those power structures.

Now, to be honest, when thinking about all of the above, there was considerable concern about diluting our message. When you're trying to serve all these different minorities, there's a nagging worry that the campaign's cohort is spreading itself too thin by trying to address everyone's problems simultaneously. There's the danger that some people might think we're saying the equivalent of 'All Lives Matter', like the people who try to dismiss the 'Black Lives Matter' advocates (I mentioned this way back in Chapter 2 – don't tell me you've been skipping pages). So let's be clear. That is *not* what we're saying: we believe that society must change to empower the entire 96 per cent. But we can only do that by focusing on the specific issues of *each different group*. Yes, that means sometimes specifically saying 'Black' or 'Asian' instead of BAME or people of colour, or creating specific policies for 'disabled women' rather than hoping they will benefit from a general policy helping 'women', to give just two examples. Society must empower the marginalised so they have more control over every aspect of their lives, so they are not subject to the whims and vagaries of societal prejudices.

Anti-racism, anti-sexism, anti-ableism, anti-prejudice in all its forms is a good start, but this world must now look at practical ways to actively empower *anyone* who feels on the outside of the 'golden circle' whether they're Black, Brown, female, disabled, gay, trans – even if they live outside London – this is about all of us having a seat at the table – not just a privileged few.

We must be able to access all areas with power and confidence.

Looking over the last eight years of this politically charged campaign, and also the chapters of this very handsome book, we'd like to offer eight simple ways in which we could achieve the seemingly impossible. True diversity and representation *across the board* in the UK film and TV industries. (And, hey, if there are any other industries that wanna do something similar that's cool, go right ahead). We like to call it the 96 per cent majority manifesto.

This is the gift that keeps on giving that Marcus and I want to offer you, gentle reader. I hope that anyone who reads this and likes the ideas it proposes will sign up to it – or, at least, start a discussion on how we can create a better society, a place where the privileged create and provide opportunities for those less fortunate than them.

All we're looking for is a change.

Let's do it together.

12

96 PER CENT MAJORITY MANIFESTO

1. **We are the 96 per cent. We believe *we* are the majority.**
   Straight able-bodied White men living in London make up 3.5 per cent of the population. Companies, organisations and society must restructure the way they operate so they benefit and reflect everyone they serve and the environment they operate in. (Chapter 2 – Majority)

2. **We believe the best solutions are achieved together**
   No one group has a monopoly on the truth and best solutions. We arrive at better outcomes when we are *all* involved in the decision-making process. (Chapter 3 – Quotas)

3. **We believe the time is now**
   Solutions must be implemented *now* to address inequality and under-representation. The wait for

a more equal society and better representation for all has been far too long. (Chapter 4 – Grey Rhino)

4. We believe in the power of allies

People in positions of privilege and influence must demonstrate how they actively support others to address inequality. (Chapter 5 – Scared)

5. We believe in individuality

Those in power must recognise that we are all human beings and not just convenient boxes to be ticked. As individuals we demand recognition, and for our *true* potential to be realised and rewarded. (Chapter 6 – More Than Numbers; and Chapter 8.5 – Loneliness)

6. We believe in structural change

Structural solutions solve systemic problems. We are fighting against cosmetic changes that have no substantive impact. We reject lip service and demand real engagement (Chapter 7 – Fake Diversity)

7. We believe in setting specific measurable goals
   All goals and targets must be measurable in order
   for those in charge to be held accountable. There
   must be tangible consequences if the objectives
   are not met. (Chapter 8 – Humpty Dumpty)

**8. We are fighting for a power share, *not* a power
   grab**
   This is not just a battle to erase the symptoms
   of all forms of prejudice. We demand a fundamental change in the status quo, an equal share
   and access to real power and how it is distributed
   throughout society. Whether you're a company,
   an organisation or a publicly funded institution,
   these issues concern you. So what are you going
   to do about it?

•

Thank you for reading this.
   Now let's get to work.

FIN

NOTES

Chapter 1

11   *less than 7 per cent of police officers* Home Office, 'Police Workforce', Ethnicity Facts and Figures, 4 Oct. 2019, https://www.ethnicity-facts-figures.service.gov.uk/workforce-and-business/workforce-diversity/police-workforce/latest

11   *Less than 10 per cent of British teachers* Home Office, 'School Teacher Workforce', Ethnicity Facts and Figures, 28 Jan. 2020, https://www.ethnicity-facts-figures.service.gov.uk/workforce-and-business/workforce-diversity/school-teacher-workforce/latest#by-ethnicity-and-role

11   *six female chief executives* Equality Trust, 'Fat Cat Friday 2019: Only Six FTSE CEOs are Women and they Earn 54% of the Salaries of Male Counterparts', 4 Jan. 2019, https://www.equalitytrust.org.uk/news/fat-cat-friday-2019-only-six-ftse-ceos-are-women-and-they-earn-54-salaries-male-counterparts

11   *65 per cent went to private school* The Sutton
     Trust and the Social Mobility Commission,
     'Elitist Britain: The Educational Backgrounds
     of Britain's Leading People', 2019, p. 6, https://
     www.suttontrust.com/our-research/elitist-
     britain-2019/

11   *7 per cent of the population receive a private*
     education Sutton Trust, 'Elitist Britain', p. 4.

Chapter 3

26   *hideously middle class* Jasper Jackson, 'TV
     Industry is "Hideously Middle Class", says
     Endemol Shine's Tim Hincks', *Guardian*, 1
     July 2015, https://www.theguardian.com/
     media/2015/jul/01/tv-industry-middle-class-
     endemol-shine-tim-hincks-diversity

26   *higher managerial and professional*
     job Dermot Feenan, 'Is the BBC Hideously
     Middle Class?', *Open Democracy*, 17 Oct. 2017,
     https://www.opendemocracy.net/en/ourbeeb/
     is-bbc-hideously-middle-class/

27   *non-selective, state schools* Ofcom, 'Breaking
     the Class Ceiling: Social Make-up of the TV
     Industry Revealed', 18 Sept. 2019, https://www.

ofcom.org.uk/about-ofcom/latest/media/media-releases/2019/breaking-the-class-ceiling-tv-industry-social-makeup-revealed

33   *your taste in music* David Brooks, 'Getting Radical About Inequality', *New York Times*, 18 July 2017

37   *Norway has specific laws* 'Quotas to Gender-Balance the Board: Norway's Drastic Action Worked', *Ideas for Leaders*, 602, April 2016, https://www.ideasforleaders.com/ideas/quotas-to-gender-balance-the-board-norway%E2%80%99s-drastic-action-worked

Chapter 3.5

44   *direct correlation between companies* Broadcast Equality and Training Regulator, *Training and Skills and Equal Opportunities Report 2010*, July 2011

45   *Akerlof* 'George A. Akerlof', Library of Economics and Liberty, 2018, https://www.econlib.org/library/Enc/bios/Akerlof.html

Chapter 4

50   *switching off terrestrial British television*
      Digital-i, *Mind The Viewing Gap: An Industry
      Report on Ethnic Diversity*, Nov. 2017

52   *grey rhino* 'The Gray Rhino' [press release],
      https://www.wucker.com/writing/the-gray-rhino/

53   *By 2031* Philip Rees et al., 'Ethnic Population
      Projections for the UK and Local Areas,
      2011–2061: New Results for the Fourth
      Demographic Transition', Presentation at the
      British Society for Population Studies, Annual
      Conference, Leeds, 7–9 Sept. 2015, https://
      www.ethpop.org/Presentations/NewETHPOP/
      BSPS2015/BSPS%20Ethnic%20Population%20
      Projections%20Phil%20Rees.pdf

55   *Choosing the wrong response* Michele Wucker,
      'From Black Swans to Gray Rhinos: How to
      Stop Overlooking Obvious Risks', *LinkedIn
      Pulse*, 2 Sept. 2016, https://www.linkedin.com/
      pulse/from-black-swans-gray-rhinos-how-stop-
      overlooking-obvious-wucker/

58   *Between 2006 and 2012* Creative Skillset,
      'Employment Census of the Creative Media
      Industries', 2012, https://www.screenskills.

com/media/1552/2012_employment_census_
of_the_creative_media_industries.pdf

Chapter 5

69   *A seminal paper* Michelle Duguid,
     'Female Tokens in High-prestige Work
     Groups: Catalysts or Inhibitors of Group
     Diversification?', *Organizational Behavior
     and Human Decision Processes*, 116/1, Sept.
     2011, 104–15, https://doi.org/10.1016/j.
     obhdp.2011.05.009

70   *Women and non-White executives* Courtney
     Connley, 'Are Minorities Penalized for
     Promoting Diversity in the Workplace?',
     Black Enterprise, 11 April 2016, https://www.
     blackenterprise.com/are-minorities-penalized-
     for-promoting-diversity/

70   *Race and Self-Presentation in the Labor
     Market* Sonia K. Kang et al., 'Whitened
     Résumés: Race and Self-Presentation
     in the Labor Market', *Administrative
     Science Quarterly*, 61/3, 1 Sept. 2016,
     469–502, https://journals.sagepub.com/doi/
     abs/10.1177/0001839216639577

75 *Lenny Henry was very critical* Culture, Media
    and Sport Committee, 'Oral Evidence: Future
    of the BBC', HC 315, 15 July 2014, Q660,
    http://data.parliament.uk/writtenevidence/
    committeeevidence.svc/evidencedocument/
    culture-media-and-sport-committee/future-of-
    the-bbc/oral/11461.html

79 *championing diversity can be beneficial* Bourree
    Lam, 'A Workplace-Diversity Dilemma', *The
    Atlantic*, 7 April 2016

Chapter 6

81 *14 per cent* 'Women make up just 13.6% of
    film directors in the UK', *BBC News*, 5 May
    2016

81 *1 per cent* Directors UK, *Adjusting the Colour
    Balance: Black, Asian and Minority Ethnic
    Representation Among Screen Directors
    Working in UK Television*, September 2018

89 *Any Questions?* http://www.bbc.co.uk/
    programmes/b006qgvj

89 *Black British people are vastly over-
    represented in mental health statistics* http://
    www.mind.org.uk/help/people_groups_and_

communities/statistics_3_race_culture_and_
mental_health

89   *three times more likely to be admitted to British psychiatric hospitals* John Carvel, 'Black people three times as likely to be in mental hospital', *Guardian*, 7 Dec. 2005, https://www.theguardian.com/society/2005/dec/07/socialcare.raceintheuk

89   *self-discrepancy* http://en.wikipedia.org/wiki/Self-Discrepancy_Theory

89   *this prejudice is nearly always indirect* http://issuu.com/helixwebsites/docs/televisionsept11-redact

90   *2.5 times more likely to suffer from depression* Kristen Bellstrom, 'Depressed? Anxious? Blame the Gender Pay Gap', *Fortune*, 7 Jan. 2016, http://fortune.com/2016/01/07/depression-anxiety-pay-gap/

90   *a clear link between being the victim of racial discrimination at work and a range of mental health issues* 'Examining the Link Between Racism and Health', *Psychology Today*, 19 Oct. 2017, https://www.psychologytoday.com/intl/blog/evidence-based-living/201710/examining-the-link-between-racism-and-health

90   *sharing common experiences* https://
      ie.reachout.com/getting-help-2/face-to-face-
      help/things-you-need-to-know/benefits-of-
      talking-to-someone/

Chapter 7

96   *a Google employee* Hassan A. Kanu, 'Google
      Uses "Bait and Switch" in Diversity Hires,
      Worker Alleges', *Bloomberg Law*, 9 May
      2019, https://news.bloomberglaw.com/daily-
      labor-report/google-uses-bait-and-switch-in-
      diversity-hires-worker-alleges

97   *photoshopping two women* Ryan Mac, 'This
      Picture Featuring 15 Tech Men And 2
      Women Looked Doctored. The Women Were
      Photoshopped In.', *BuzzFeed News*, 12 June
      2019, https://www.buzzfeednews.com/article/
      ryanmac/tech-titans-women-fake-photoshop-
      cucinelli-gq

100   *how many directors at the major broadcasters
      were people of colour* Directors UK,
      'Directors of Colour', https://www.directors.
      uk.com/campaigns/bame-directors

Chapter 8

106 *twenty-nine schemes* Barnie Choudhury, 'Still Hideously White?', *Open Democracy*, 18 Dec. 2013, https://www.opendemocracy.net/en/ourbeeb/still-hideously-white/

110 *its definition* Ofcom, *Regional Production and Regional Programme Definitions: Guidance for Public Service Broadcasters*, 6 Jan. 2010, https://www.ofcom.org.uk/__data/assets/pdf_file/0019/87040/Regional-production-and-regional-programme-definitions.pdf

111 *two-tick system* Channel 4, *360° Diversity Charter: Two Years On*, 27 Feb. 2017, http://www.channel4.com/media/documents/corporate/26509_C4_DiversityReport2017_FINAL_27.02.17.pdf

112 *three-tick system* 'The Quality of Difference: BFI Celebrates Diversity' [press release], 15 Oct. 2015, https://www.bfi.org.uk/sites/bfi.org.uk/files/downloads/bfi-press-release-bfi-announces-%C2%A31m-diversity-fund-new-standards-film-fund-projects-2015-10-15.pdf

112 *they were ring-fencing money to develop diverse productions* Culture, Media and Sport

Committee, 'Oral Evidence: Future of the BBC'.

112 *nurture talent* BBC Commissioning, 'Creative Diversity Development Fund Launched', 01 Sept. 2014, https://www.bbc. co.uk/commissioning/news/articles/creative-diversity-development-fund-launched

114 *'clear targets'* 'Letter from Sadiq Khan to Ofcom's Sharon White', *Observer*, 1 Oct. 2017, https://www.theguardian.com/world/2017/ sep/30/sadiq-khan-letter-sharon-white-ofcom-bame

Chapter 8.5

123 *more at risk of suffering from lone-liness* Simon Antrobus et al., 'Alone in the Crowd: Loneliness and Diversity', Calouste Gulbenkian Foundation, 2015, http:// www.gulbenkian.org.uk/publications/ publications/112-Alone-in-the-crowd-loneliness-and-diversity.html

124 *'people who are lonely'* Claire Zillman, 'Being Lonely at Work is Bad for Business', *Fortune*, 29 July 2014, https://fortune.com/2014/07/29/ worker-loneliness/

124 *'co-workers can recognise'* Hakan Ozcelik
and Sigal Barsade, 'Work Loneliness and
Employee Performance', 30 Jan. 2012,
https://faculty.wharton.upenn.edu/wp-
content/uploads/2012/05/Work_Loneliness_
Performance_Study.pdf

Chapter 9

131 *26.4 per cent* Stephen Follows, 'What
Percentage of Film Producers are Women?', 15
April 2019, https://stephenfollows.com/what-
percentage-of-film-producers-are-women/

135 *5 per cent on average* Mark Sweney, 'UK Film
Industry on a Roll as It Helps Keep Economy
Growing', Guardian, 26 July 2017, https://www.
theguardian.com/film/2017/jul/26/uk-film-
industry-economy-ons-movie-tv-tax-breaks-
pound

142 *a great study* What Works Centre for Economic
Growth, 'How to Evaluate Innovation:
UK "Creative Credits" Programme', https://
whatworksgrowth.org/resources/how-to-
evaluate-innovation-case-study-uk-creative-
credits-programme-randomi/